FIELD SPORTS LIBRARY

Ferreting and Trapping for Amateur Gamekeepers

Other Books by the Author

Gamekeeping and Shooting for Amateurs

Ratting and Rabbiting for
Amateur Gamekeepers

Ferreting and Trapping for Amateur Gamekeepers

By
GUY N. SMITH

Photographs by Lance Smith
Drawings by Pat Lakin

NIMROD PRESS LTD
PO Box 1
Liss, Hants
England

ISBN 0-947647-47-3

First Printed Jan. 1978
Second Edition 1979
Third Edition 1986

Printer: R J Acford
Chichester
W. Sussex

NIMROD PRESS LTD
Liss, Hants

This book is dedicated to the late Frank Hurcombe, one of the real old warreners

Acknowledgments

BRIAN and TREVOR MORRIS for their help and co-operation.

PAT LAKIN for hours of painstaking work in compiling the many drawings.

Messrs A. FENN, High Street, Astwood Bank, Redditch Worcs. for their co-operation in supplying information regarding humane vermin and rabbit traps.

DAVID CLUETT for photographs.

LANCE SMITH who also supplied photographs.

CONTENTS

		Page
	Introduction	1
	Part One: Ferreting	5
Chapter		
1	The Ferret and its relatives	7
2	Ferret Management	29
3	The Quarry	45
4	Training and Working Ferrets to Rabbits and Rats	61
5	Alternative Methods of Rabbit Control and some advice on Ratting	91
	Part Two: Trapping	105
6	The Trapper's Qua[illegible]	107
7	Traps and Trapping	129
	Index	158

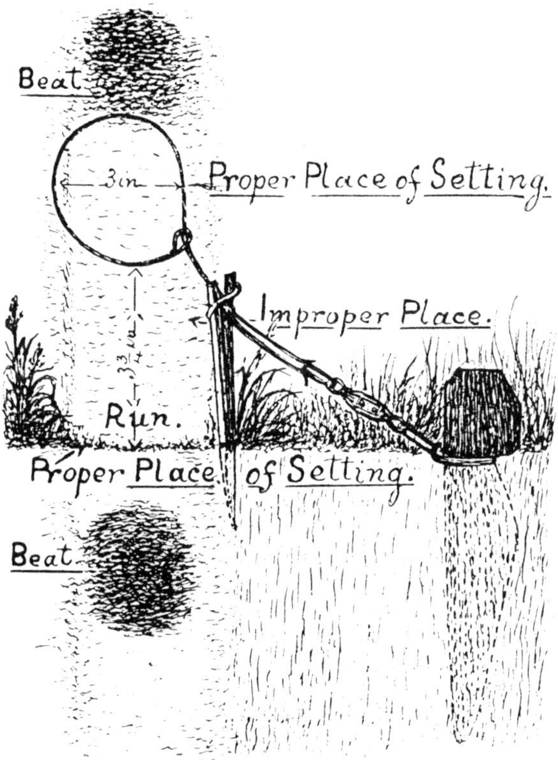

The Rabbit Snare
This must be set before or after the beat (flat place made by the jumps of the animals)

Introduction

The role of the amateur gamekeeper is not restricted solely to forays with the gun after vermin and the rearing of pheasants. Indeed, these duties only comprise part of his extremely busy year.

Most shooting rights which are properly leased contain a clause to the effect that the tenant is responsible for the damage done by rabbits to growing crops and forestry. Since the advent of myxamatosis this has been purely a technical clause presenting no real worrry to the shooting man. However, within the last two or three years it has become increasingly obvious to all connected with rural pursuits that the rabbit is making a determined comeback in almost every part of the British Isles. Whilst there are reports that some rabbits are living above ground (one fact that is attributed to the decline of the disease, in so much that the fleas which spread it are not able to transfer themselves from one rabbit to another away from the close confinement of a burrow), we can be reasonably certain that they do spend a large proportion of their lives below ground.

The days of the professional warrener are over. He has been replaced by the "man from the Ministry", in most cases armed solely with a tin of Cymag rabbit-gas. It is arguable that this method of control is wasteful in times of soaring meat prices and food shortage. The author and his family eat at least one rabbit per week and, with some thought given to preparation and cooking, the diet never becomes monotonous.

We, the shooting men of today, are a new breed of warreners. Ferrets, nets and guns are our basic equipment. The close of the game-shooting season does not mean that we must wait another seven months until our sport begins again. We shall benefit by transferring our attention to the warrens, and in so doing we shall cement a relationship with our landlords whether they be farmers or forestry owners.

Yet, some knowledge is essential before we commence learning by experience. Otherwise we shall return home empty-handed, disillusioned and our ferrets will suffer hardships because of our ignorance in their management.

One purpose of this book is to teach the beginner how to keep and work ferrets. The other is to provide a guide to vermin-control, apart from the casual walk round with the gun in the hope of an odd stoat or weasel showing itself. Every shoot has a population of ground vermin, the vast majority of which are never seen by the amateur gamekeeper. Indeed, in many cases the novice is probably unaware of their presence and is puzzled concerning the lack of game on shooting days, knowing that he reared and turned out a full quota of birds and patrolled his ground regularly.

Stoats, weasels, rats, grey squirrels, etc., will slowly and surely decimate a population of game. Hours can be wasted in waiting patiently at a suitable place with the gun. We may shoot one, perhaps two, of our four-footed foes, but for each killed a score or more will evade us.

Only a properly maintained network of traps will combat ground vermin efficiently on a shoot. Yet, a hundred traps to the acre will be useless if sited badly or not set properly. The old maxim that "a trap never eats anything and it doesn't mind waiting" is certainly true, and it is hoped that the amateur keeper will benefit from the advice given in this book, and that it will prove to be a solid foundation upon which to build from practical experience.

Ferreting and trapping must be regarded as allied methods in helping to maintain the balance of Nature.

Setting out, fully equipped, for a day's ferreting

Part One: FERRETING

CHAPTER 1

The Ferret and its Relatives

HISTORY OF THE FERRET

The ferret is a native of Africa. Centuries ago it was imported into Spain for the purpose of reducing the numbers of rabbits with which that country was over-run. From there it spread to the rest of Europe, not in its original wild state, however, but as a domesticated animal. From very early times the ferret has been used as a means of bolting rabbits from their burrows—the usual method being to turn it muzzled into a warren.

The original colour of the ferret is a yellowish white. Brown specimens are those of a mixed breed which incorporate the polecat, but in order to understand fully this animal which we shall be keeping, breeding and working, it is necessary to make a brief study of its relatives.

THE WEASEL

The weasel is the smallest member of the ferret family, and is easily distinguished from the stoat by the fact that it has no black tip on its tail. The upper parts of the body are a reddish brown whilst the lower regions are light coloured. There is a white spot below the corners of the mouth, the eyes are black and the ears are small and rounded. The male is 8 in. long, including its 2 in. tail, and stands some 2½ in. high. The female is approximately 1½ in. shorter.

The weasel is nocturnal by nature, but sometimes

The Weasel—A determined hunter

hunts during the day as well. For its size it is the fiercest of all British mammals, and has been known frequently to attack a foe several times larger than itself. It is apparently without fear, but this does not detract from its cunning. It recognises Man as an enemy and will dart into cover at his approach. There are records of weasels having been seen hunting in packs, but these must be regarded as isolated instances.

Its main diet consists of voles, moles, frogs and small birds, but it will tackle rats and poultry. Most of its victims are killed by biting through the base of the neck or else severing the jugular vein. It has been known to hang on to a fully grown cockerel until the bird finally succumbed to its attacks.

The weasel hunts by scent, and can both swim and climb trees if the occasion demands. Overall it is an excellent vermin-killer, but its occasional ravages in the game-preserves puts it on the gamekeeper's "wanted" list.

Apart from Man its only real other enemy is the bird of prey. Whilst the kestrel is mostly content to confine its attentions to mice and voles, the sparrow-hawk may strike like a bolt from the blue; or the buzzard which has waited patiently, motionless and almost invisible in the lower boughs of a dead tree, will drop suddenly on to the unsuspecting weasel.

Yet, the weasel knows a few tricks of its own, as those of us who have watched its "dance of death" are fully aware. The creature often chooses the area around a bird-table in a residential garden as the stage for its "show". At its approach the birds fly up into the nearby trees. It appears not to notice them, being more concerned with a continuous performance of acrobatics, turning and twisting this way and that. The feathered audience become curious and a few of them fly down for a closer view. Still the weasel is apparently unaware of their presence. Soon it is surrounded by a circle of astonished birds, and now its antics are taking it closer and closer to them. Then, in one brief moment the climax is reached, and all the birds except the unfortunate victim fly off in alarm. The weasel's hypnotic spell is broken, but the sparrows and blackbirds have short memories. Within a matter of hours they are capable of being fooled by an identical performance.

The weasel's lair is usually to be found in either a hollow tree or a hole in a bank. The female has a litter of between four and six young in the spring, and sometimes breeds a second time, particularly if an accident befalls the first batch of young. If danger threatens she will move them to a place of greater safety, carrying one a few yards, putting it down, and going back for another until the relay is complete, and the whole litter is installed in another nest. This is no debatable point, as is the case of the female woodcock carrying her young, for the writer has witnessed it at first hand.

In colder climates the fur of the weasel turns a lighter colour, pure white in areas where snow lies for long periods, and this change takes place within a few hours, governed by the fall in atmospheric temperature. White weasels have been recorded in Britain, in both 1947 and 1963 when severe weather conditions persisted for several weeks. With the advent of cold weather it moves closer to human habitation, often taking up residence in farm outbuildings. Once one spent two whole months in a crevice in a suburban rockery, and the lady of the house was in the habit of putting out food scraps daily for it. However, this heralded danger for the local bird population, and she would often disturb its ritual of acrobatic enticement by banging loudly on the window when the weasel was within striking distance of the nearest bird.

The weasel is a member of the *genus mustela* (stoat, otter, skunk, pine marten, badger, sable, wolverine) all of which are valuable fur-bearers. The glands secreting the obnoxious fluid are controlled by the animal, but are only totally repulsive in the case of the skunk and the polecat. The others eject a fluid which simply has a strong musky odour, and is not sufficient to repel an enemy.

The weasel is very versatile and is capable of climbing trees in search of small birds or swimming in streams after water-voles. Often it is wrongfully blamed for the depredations of the stoat, its closest cousin and a much more indiscriminate killer.

The weasel is probably the most likeable of the whole species apart from the ferret itself, although there are only one or two isolated instances of domestication. One was once kept in captivity by a French lady, named Mademoiselle de Laistre, who kept it in her bedroom. During the daytime it slept on a quilt, but at night it was locked in a cage. She found it most affectionate, and her only complaint was that it squeaked most of the night during the summer months. Possibly this had a bearing on its urge to mate. She claimed that it could distinguish her voice amidst twenty others in the room. Of course, it emitted those musky odours at times, but these she dispelled with perfume!

THE STOAT

The stoat is larger than the weasel, about 14 in. long including a 5 in. tail. The similarity between stoat and

The Stoat—Concentrates on larger prey

The Polecat—Carries an obnoxious odour

An ideal place for a stoat to make its home, a bank with additional cover due to tree-felling

weasel is great, except that the former concentrates on larger prey. For instance, in one stoat's hole were found two leverets, two leverets' heads, two young partridges and a pheasant's egg. This alone gives a good idea of its depredations.

The tip of the tail is black, and even in cold climates when the fur turns white this tuft of black hairs remains unchanged. In some areas it is known as the ermine weasel.

The snake-like movements of this animal are interesting to observe, as is the way in which it relentlessly hunts down its prey, fastening its sharp teeth into the base of its victim's neck. On one occasion during his gamekeeping duties the author came upon a stoat which had just tackled a rabbit in the manner mentioned, and killed both animals with a single shot. Like the weasel, though, the stoat atones for many of its misdeeds by killing large numbers of rats and mice, but somehow it does not have the lovable qualities of the weasel. However, one was once kept in captivity by Captain Lyon, R.N., in the last century. He had great hopes of domesticating it and took it to sea with him. Unfortunately, it was accidentally killed within the first few months, so the results of his experiment will never be known. It is reported, though, that in the initial weeks it regularly used to attempt to bite him, but eventually it consented to being stroked. This evidence suggests that it would be possible to domesticate a stoat providing that it was captivated at a very early age.

The stoat makes its hole in a bank or a hollow tree and the female breeds once only each year, giving birth to four or five young.

It is interesting to note that in Ireland a smaller species exists (*mustela hibernica*), but there are no weasels.

In 1850, 187,000 stoat skins were imported into Britain from Russia, Norway and Siberia.

POLECAT

The polecat is sometimes known as the fitch, fitchet or foumart. This animal is believed to have been used for bolting rabbits before the Roman occupation of Britain.

Much larger than either the stoat or the weasel, an adult polecat measures about 2 ft. long, including a 7 in. tail. It has long coarse fur, dark brown on the upper parts and black underneath. The head is dark with white marks about the muzzle and between the eyes and ears. It weighs about 6 lb., is a ferocious killer and is capable of climbing trees, but not with the agility of the pine marten.

The secretion from its glands, which is released when its safety is threatened, is truly obnoxious.

Usually it inhabits woodlands in hilly terrain, often within easy reach of a farm for it has a bloodthirsty craving for poultry. The writer was once invited to inspect a henhouse after a raid by a polecat. The scene had to be viewed to be believed. Twenty hens were scattered over the floor in various stages of mutilation. Only one was missing. That had been taken away for leisurely consumption! Even geese or turkeys are not safe from its depredations.

However, in the wild it has to be satisfied with whatever wild game it can find, rabbits, hares, rats, mice and small birds. Sometimes it will take fish and frogs from a stream, or even subsist on a diet of lizards and snakes.

Often its lair is at the base of a well established tree, a giant oak, for instance, in the roots of which it lives and breeds. The female has one litter per year with from three to five in number. It is recorded in Bewick's *Quadrupeds* that a polecat once caught eleven eels which were found in its hole some distance from a river during a severe winter. This, surely, illustrates the expertise of the polecat in taking fish, and as such it is an enemy of both water-bailiffs and gamekeepers who employ the common ruse of scenting their traps with musk in an effort to reduce the numbers of their enemy. However, whilst the polecat may be fairly numerous in some areas it is not sufficiently widespread to be trapped on the same scale as stoats and weasels. A bloodthirsty killer, certainly, but no true conservationist would wish it to become extinct.

PINE MARTEN

In appearance the pine marten resembles the polecat except that it has longer legs, a broader head, a sharper muzzle and a longer tail. The fur is a rich dark brown with lighter markings on throat and breast. In contrast to its other relatives it hunts by day.

At one time it was commonly known as the sweet marten—possibly this was because its secretion has merely a musky odour and is in no way as objectionable as that of the polecat.

The pine marten is undoubtedly the best climber of all—even surpassing the squirrel—using its tail as a rudder as it moves through the tree-tops, from branch to branch, with unerring balance even on the most slender boughs.

Although the pine marten does sometimes raid a game preserve, usually it contents itself with a diet of rats, mice, voles, rabbits and *soft fruits,* but its favourite food of all seems to be *frogs!* Thus we can see that it is more of a friend than a foe to the

Pine MARTEN—May be a "friend"

game-preserver.

Unfortunately the pine marten is not as abundant as most of its cousins. It is to be found in the Peak district of Derbyshire, hilly areas of Scotland and Wales, and occasionally in Ireland.

Rarely does it build its own lair, but instead renovates an old carrion crow or raven's nest, or even a squirrel's drey, high up in a tree, and inaccessible to Man. During the spring the female has a litter of four or five young.

Centuries ago pine martens were kept as pets and were found to be fairly easily tamed, and accepted domestication. However, they are unpredictable, and sometimes, for no apparent reason, get a killing urge. Possibly its closest relative is the sable of Siberia.

During the last century upwards of 100,000 skins were imported annually into Great Britain. Shooting men in the Highlands of Scotland regularly encountered the pine marten during forays after ptarmigan, and often their dogs would "tree" one. It was regarded as an enemy of game and shot on sight.

The pine marten is both inquisitive and fearless. When cornered, it arches its back like a cat, and it would be a foolish man who attempted to handle one. One report of a raid by a pine marten on a poultry farm lists two turkeys, a goose, four hens and *a cat* as its victims. Truly the killing urge was upon it then!

OTTER

The otter is the second largest of the ferret family, its size surpassed only by that of the badger. It is some 4 ft. in length, with sleek black fur, and is an excellent swimmer. The head is broad and flat, it has hairy rounded ears which close underwater, short powerful legs, sharp pointed claws with five toes on each foot,

The Otter—Can be a nuisance

and a tail which acts as a rudder.

Yet, the otter has not always been an inhabitant of the water as is evident by the fact that it has not progressed to webbed feet. The young, too, have a natural dislike of water and have to be forcibly taught to swim by their parents.

Many thousands of years ago the otter was probably a fierce hunter on land, but eventually discovered that it could make an easier living from fishing. Mostly, we associate this beautiful and mysterious creature with our native streams and rivers, but there are many more otters in the sea than ever venture inland. It must be pointed out that there is only *one* species of otter, and that the *sea-otter* is an entirely different animal altogether, more like a seal, and must not be confused with the one which we are discussing, and which has merely changed to a coastal habitat.

Sometimes the female otter will make her nest a long way from the nearest water, proof once again that the species has lived on land at some stage. However, usually she chooses a site in close proximity to a river or pool, the "holt" being a hole in a bank with an underwater entrance. Any intruder will be greeted with ferocity, for this animal is afraid of no living being, especially in the defence of her young. The author once saw a labrador dog that had been badly mauled by a female otter in these circumstances, and it was quite obvious that the scars would remain for the rest of the dog's life.

The "kits", as the otter's young are known, are blind for the first eight weeks of their lives, but by the time they are able to see they are capable of fending for themselves and earning their own living, after a few swimming lessons from their parents!

Fish are the main diet of the otter, and they have a

particular liking for salmon. Eight or ten fish constitute a meal, but like the stoat it slaughters wantonly. Consequently, it is not regarded favourably by fishermen or water-bailiffs. However, when compared with the number of salmon taken from the rivers by organised poaching gangs, the otter does very little damage, and on many occasions it actually provides sport for fishermen by moving shoals of fish that would otherwise lie-up in quiet waters.

In many areas of Great Britain the otter, like the fox, is a beast of the chase. Specially trained otter-hounds are kept for this purpose. The hunters follow their hounds at full speed along the river bank, and the air is filled with the wail of the excited dogs, the cracking of whips and the sound of the huntsman's horn. Often the much-sought after otter does not materialise, but this does not daunt the true huntsman who is already looking forward to the next meeting.

There have been various methods used for the hunting of otters over the centuries. During the 19th century a party of gentlemen, armed with flintlock guns, met regularly in a remote part of the Hebrides. Their gamekeepers used to work a pack of hounds through the rocky coastline in an attempt to flush otters out for the guns. Certainly this method was less sporting than today's, and the bag at the end of each meet was considerably higher.

About this same time a man by the name of Collins, living near Wooler in Northumberland, domesticated an otter which he used to take daily to the river to feed. One day his son undertook this task, and after a couple of hours or so the otter swam off. By nightfall it had not returned, and it was presumed that the animal had decided to return to its wild state. Each afternoon Collins, senior, went down to the river and called his pet, but there was no sign of it. Then, on the sixth day, it appeared swimming towards him, and quite happily returned to the house with him.

There is another case of a domesticated otter which was kept at Corsbie House, Wigtonshire. This particular animal had a strong liking for gooseberries!

In olden times the Roman Catholic Church used to permit the eating of otter on "maigre" days. The cooked flesh was reported as being "dark, rank and with a layer of fat beneath it". Hardly a sportsman's repast!

Should you wish to observe an otter in its natural environment then you must find one of this creature's "landing" places—perhaps a flat rock or a fallen tree beside a river bank. You will be able to tell from the tracks in the mud whether or not otters are using this place, and how frequently. Observation will not be easy, for the otter has the keenest scent and eyesight, and mostly it is a nocturnal animal. Concealment and a long wait are inevitable, but if in the end you catch a brief glimpse of this beautiful creature then the time and effort will have been well spent.

River pollution has been detrimental to our inland otter population this last decade, and it has forced them to change their haunts. Polluted rivers mean an absence of fish, and the otter will travel far afield in search of its natural food. Perhaps this will mean that those otters which have spent their lives hunting inland rivers and streams will turn to the shore for their living, and then we shall stand even less chance of viewing them.

The East Anglian Broads are another favourite habitat of the otter where these animals live in the extensive reed-beds. In times of drought the otter can sometimes be seen travelling across land as the waterways which adjoin the separate pools have dried up. It moves at an amazing speed on terra firma, and has been known to cover several miles in one night.

The otter quickly adapts to a change of diet when it is forced to seek refuge on the coast. It makes its holt in some secluded cave, accessible only from the sea, and will hunt the rock pools in search of crabs, small fish and mussels. Eels are a delicacy that are mostly to be found in the autumn at the mouths of tidal rivers as they make their way to winter in the sea.

The male otter is exceedingly jealous during the mating season, and often will engage in battle with a rival from which only the winner will emerge alive. He is a good parent, though, guarding the nest and hunting to provide food for the young.

However, the pairing is only temporary, lasting until the young are able to fend for themselves. From that moment onwards the male and female show no interest in each other, and separate to go their own ways.

The otter is an asset to any stretch of water, a reminder to us that there are still truly wild tracts remaining in this overcrowded island of ours.

BADGER

Finally, we come to the badger, the largest of the family, and although in many ways it is far removed from the stoat and weasel in bloodthirsty ferocity, we cannot leave Brock out. It must be emphasised, though, that this animal is now protected by law, and that since 25th January 1974, it has been illegal to take or kill badgers without a special licence. The days of the so-called "sport" of badger-digging are over.

Linnaeus and other naturalists have likened the badger to the bear. Some compare it with the pig,

Brock the Badger—A fascinating animal

referring to the adults as "boar" and "sow" but, nevertheless, it is one of the weasel tribe, and as such must be included in this chapter.

An adult badger is some 2½–3 ft. in length, stands about 1 ft. high and weighs between 35 and 40 lb. The body is stocky and powerful, with a pointed muzzle. Whether or not the reader has actually seen one, he will no doubt be familiar with this grey and black creature with the striped head, a favourite subject for many artists in children's books.

Brock, as he is known throughout the British Isles, is really a peace loving creature and asks no more than to be left to his own devices. His food consists of young rabbits, voles, frogs, hedgehogs, mice, snakes, wasps, acorns and a variety of roots. Indeed, he is more of an ally to the gamekeeper, and it is only the old "rogue" who can no longer forage for his own food who succumbs to the temptation of killing young pheasant poults in covert.

Brock constructs his "sett" as far from human habitation as possible, and often these underground warrens in some remote wood will occupy as much as a quarter of an acre of land. He has no objection to parts of his spacious home being shared by either rabbits or foxes, and on occasion this happens. Reynard is often grateful for the deeper tunnellings of his landlord which enable him to evade a pursuing pack of hounds.

The badger is the cleanest of animals, and if one examines the ground carefully in the vicinity of a well-used sett one will doubtless find a track disappearing into the undergrowth. On following this one will come upon a clearing where badger droppings are much in evidence. This is the toilet, well away from the living quarters.

The badger does not hibernate, although during

prolonged spells of severe weather it will retire to the very depths of the maze of warrens it inhabits, and sleep until the climate becomes milder. It has a curious habit of sucking a claw whilst sleeping, in the same manner which a young child employs.

When seeking a badger sett, this can often be located in an area of woodland where the lower parts of the tree-trunks have been scored by the animals sharpening their claws. However, having found the sett, unless one is prepared to endure a long nocturnal vigil in the branches of a nearby tree, one is unlikely to obtain a glimpse of the occupants. It is best to choose the time of a full moon, when success will entail continual silence, and no smoking.

In spring the sow gives birth to three or four young. The boar is a good father, helping to forage for food to feed the "earth pigs" as they are sometimes called. Badgers mate for life, and it is seldom that either partner deserts the other. Perhaps the human race could do worse than take a leaf out of Brock's humble book!

Those who take up ferreting may well come across a badger from time to time. In no way will this creature be detrimental to your sport, and he has inherited his right to hunt those woods over the years. The very same sett which he occupies was probably occupied by badgers a score or more years ago.

Bovine TB in Badgers

One factor which must not be overlooked is that badgers carry and spread bovine tuberculosis. Infected badgers have been discovered in Avon, Cornwall, Devon, Dorset, Gloucestershire and Wiltshire. This has resulted in humane control, infected setts being gassed by Ministry officials. In 1975, 958 cattle reacted to the TB test in 386 herds in the West Country, whilst as a result of Ministry efforts concerning infected setts only 550 cattle in 285 herds reacted in the first nine months of 1976. The public were invited to submit any badger carcases for examination, and as a result infection was located in Surrey and East Sussex.

The total badger population of Britain is estimated to be in the region of 90,000, and all areas cleared by the Ministry are likely to re-populate themselves quickly. In fact, steps have to be taken to prevent this for a time after gassing has been carried out. At the moment it is not known whether complete clearance of badgers in an infected area will bring about the total removal of bovine TB.

Gassing badger setts has been carried out by the Ministry of Agriculture since the spring of 1976, but the early efforts were not a success due to the dry weather at that time. Details of gassing are explained in a later chapter dealing with rabbit control by this means. Many badger setts had to be re-gassed on account of the initial failure, but eventually it was proved to be a success. Between 1970 and 1976, in Dorset 626 cattle had to be slaughtered, but the onslaught on setts is already reducing this figure considerably on average.

The Ministry strongly urge that all gassing as a means of control, whether badgers or rabbits, is left to Ministry officials.

CHAPTER 2

Ferret Management

Although the ferret is a bloodthirsty creature, if looked after properly it will be as docile as most pets. However, it is as well to point out at the very beginning that under no circumstances should children be allowed to undertake this task. **Ferrets are not hamsters or guinea-pigs.** If ill-treated or mishandled they will bite, and they are capable of inflicting a wound as deep as the bone in your finger. Almost everybody who has kept ferrets will relate the occasion on which they were bitten, but it is almost a certainty that in nine cases out of ten the fault lay with themselves.

BUYING YOUR FIRST FERRET

Some thought must be given to the purchase of your first ferret. Almost every sporting, rural and livestock publication carries advertisements for ferrets, but it is as well to go and look at a few in your own locality before finally making your choice. It is unwise to buy an adult one without making some enquiries into its background. The vendor who claims that you are buying the best ferret in the district, with several commendable working seasons behind it, may well have an ulterior motive in disposing of it. Perhaps it has become lazy, or else developed the habit of lying up with every rabbit it kills. You could, of course, pick up a bargain. It may be that the seller is giving up rabbiting, and wishes his ferrets to go to a good home where they will be guaranteed plenty of work. Always examine your intended purchase thoroughly to ensure that it is not suffering from some ailment. In this same chapter are given the diseases which are most common to these creatures, and it would be advisable to familiarise yourself with the various symptoms so that you will be able to identify them. The last thing you want to do is to start off with a sick ferret.

It is best to begin with two ferrets, but *not* a breeding pair. Otherwise you will be attempting too much in the early stages. Learn to manage and work your animals before launching into breeding.

Like almost every other creature, ferrets like company. A solitary one will suffer from loneliness and boredom, and you cannot expect it to work at its best. A couple of jills (females) are preferable to two hobs (males). The former are less inclined to fight than the latter, although often this depends upon the individuals, their surroundings and your own attitude towards them. A couldn't-care-less approach by the owner will result in irritable lazy ferrets.

So you have decided upon two jills. Now all that remains is to choose between white or polecat, and large or small. It is purely a matter of personal choice, but bear in mind that white ferrets are more easily spotted when they emerge from a rabbit bury and wander off amongst dense undergrowth. Also, if you have a careless or impetuous shot accompanying you on a rabbiting expedition, a white ferret is less likely to be shot accidentally than a darker one. Of course, steps should be taken beforehand to ensure that only safe guns are present, but there are always those embarrassing occasions when a friend-of-a-friend turns up, usually without being invited. The remedy is not to invite the original friend next time!

Your choice at this stage is a white jill. Large or small? One point to remember is that a small ferret can often get round a rabbit in a dead-end burrow

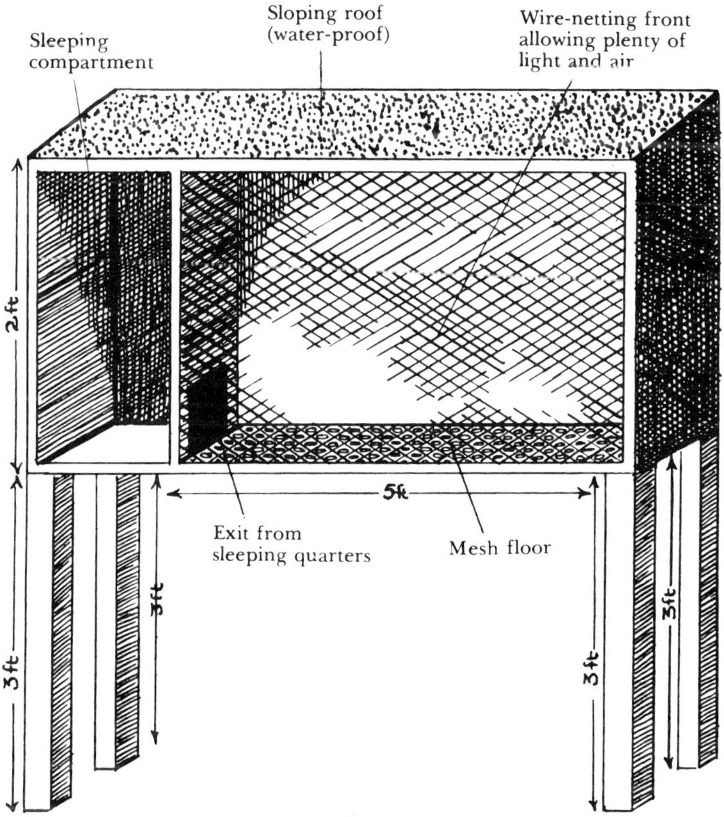

DESIGN FOR A FERRET HUTCH

and move it, whilst a large one is inclined to scratch at the rabbit's rear and lie-up with it, thereby causing you time and effort in digging. You will certainly learn how to dig with a large ferret working for you, but in the early stages it might be advisable to gain experience without laborious time-wasting.

You have now bought your first ferrets, two small white jills, and if you are to get the best out of them, and not become disillusioned with this aspect of the sport of shooting, time and trouble must be taken over their quarters. They must have ample room, be warm and dry, and, above all, be fed correctly and *kept clean.*

THE HUTCH

An outhouse is not always the best place for a ferret-hutch. All too often it is dark and inclined to become damp even with the door left open. Ferrets like an airy situation, and far better is it that they are kept out-of-doors so long as the hutch is in a reasonably sheltered place out of the wind. A moveable structure is best so that its position can be altered in accordance with weather conditions. A corner of a patio or yard which catches the sun is ideal.

A Guide to Making a Hutch

In order to maintain healthy ferrets dampness must be avoided at all times. Consequently, the hutch should be a couple of feet or so off the ground, well-ventilated and allowing ample sunlight. It should consist of two separate compartments, one for sleeping and the other for playing and eating in. You will need a second smaller hutch in order to segregate your animals if one becomes sick, and also for use when you decide to breed, when it is necessary to remove the jill from the hob.

Let us consider the type of hutch which should suit the beginner and can easily be made by someone who has very little knowledge of carpentry. It should be at least 3 ft. long, 2 ft. wide and 2 ft. deep. An old trestle-table is ideal on which to stand it, but ensure that this is sound and not likely to collapse.

The floor must drain easily, and this can either be metal and sloping, or else wire mesh so that the foulings drop through. In the latter case it is best if your hutch is a complete structure on 2 ft. supports, allowing the excreta to fall to the ground beneath. All too many ferret-hutches are nothing more than stout wooden boxes with separate compartments—as a result cleaning-out is difficult and the urine soaks into the wooden floor. It will not be long before the hutch has an unpleasant smell and the ferrets develop a number of ailments. Many of the warreners of old kept their ferrets under terrible conditions, and it was due mostly to this that the ferret earned itself an unsavoury reputation. It was the owners who were to blame—if cared for properly the ferret is neither smelly nor vicious.

If, however, the floor of your hutch is wooden, then a sand-tray is essential. The sand should be changed daily, or certainly every other day.

Heavy water and food containers are advised. Light ones are apt to become overturned. Food will be trodden into the floor and wasted, and your ferrets may go thirsty for long periods through having upset their water. Likewise, containers must be washed before being refilled. No uneaten food should be left on the floor. Sand is always preferable to sawdust on the floor. It does not become saturated, and neither does it cling to the fur of the ferrets.

Waterproof roofing material is essential if the hutch is out of doors. Tarpaulin is probably the best to use, and it will last for years. A slanting roof is important otherwise puddles will form which will run off in all directions every time you open the lid. A hinged roof will certainly make life considerably easier for yourself.

All the framework should be on the outside of the hutch leaving the insides a smooth surface. The benefit of this will be easier cleaning-out and more room for your ferrets.

The sleeping-quarters should be cleaned out at least twice a week and replenished with fresh hay or straw. It is a good idea to sprinkle insect powder on the bedding as a precaution against fleas.

These directions, together with the accompanying diagram, will enable you to construct a serviceable hutch that should meet the requirements of your first attempts at ferret management. However, having persevered successfully for some months you may decide that you are now qualified to look after more than a couple of jills, and in this case your needs will be best served by the construction of a ferret-court.

FERRET-COURTS

A ferret-court is a large structure in which are situated a number of separate compartments, the occupants of which all share the same run-out. It is the equivalent of a row of terraced houses sharing a communual yard. However, separate run-outs can also be made within this enclosure, again like terraced houses with their own gardens enclosed within the communal yard.

The object of the court is to keep the ferrets apart where large numbers are confined under one roof. Jills on heat and sick animals can be kept in solitary

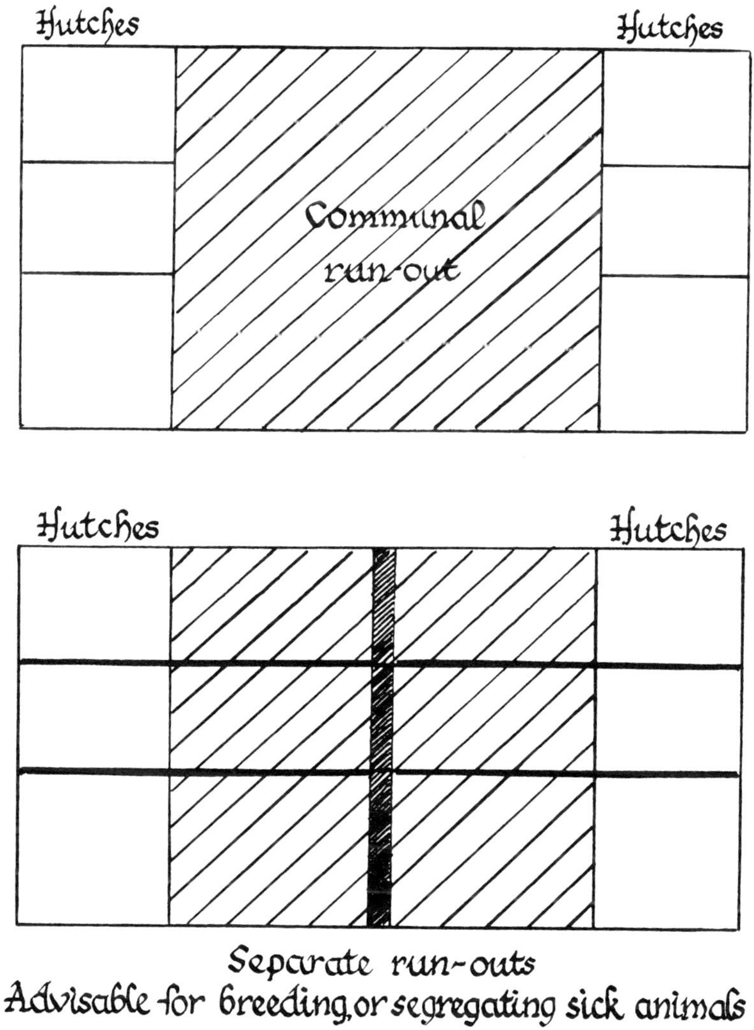

DIAGRAM OF FERRET-COURTS

confinement. A barn or a large outhouse is ideal for a ferret-court.

Whilst the animals require no less attention than in hutches, it means that they can be supervised, fed, and cleaned-out as a whole much easier.

Ferret-courts are not widely used today. Some of the old warreners housed their animals in one, but possibly lack of space in modern dwellings has caused them to be discontinued in preference for a number of separate hutches. If you have the space available then a court is advisable. Much time will be saved each week, and the diagram shows a proposed lay-out for an elementary structure.

FEEDING

Any old table scraps are just not good enough for your ferrets. The correct diet is essential for healthy working ferrets, and there are a variety of conflicting ideas on this subject.

A Flesh Diet

First, the ferret is carnivorous by nature, and as such it is important to feed it on flesh. Too many are mistakenly fed regularly on bread and milk.

Ferrets prefer their meat given to them as they would find it in the wild, i.e., rabbits in their fur and birds in feather. Those who hunt rabbits regularly should keep back a proportion of their kills with which to feed their ferrets. In these modern times a supply can be kept in a deep-freeze. Woodpigeons, poultry heads and entrails will also be ravenously devoured, but when supplies are short "lights" or scraps can usually be obtained from a butcher for a few pence.

Over-feeding

Do not over-feed. It is best to feed ferrets twice a day and see that they are not allowed to gorge themselves. As mentioned before, all uneaten food should be removed from the hutch or court. As a rule ferrets will devour their quota within a few minutes, and any that are reluctant to eat should be examined as this is an indication that they are not in good health.

They should be given a little milk, preferably with the morning feed, but *fresh water must always be available.*

There is much controversy over the subject of working "hungry" ferrets. Many of the old warreners advocated working a starving animal, but this school of thought has now been generally disregarded. An unfed ferret is more likely to lie up with its kill. A far better idea is to feed your ferrets an hour or so earlier than usual on rabbiting days, and also to give them a smaller quantity. In this way they will be neither ravenous nor sluggish, and much "digging time" will be saved.

Before the last war there was a gamekeeper living in the Midlands who kept a couple of ferrets. These were reserved for his Sunday morning outings when he used to rely upon a score or so of rabbits to supplement his meagre wages. However, from Monday to Saturday they received but scant attention, and he was accustomed to throwing into the hutch any dead item of vermin from his rounds. These ferrets lived in squalour, and as such were both evil-smelling and vicious. One day he came upon a dead heron which he immediately saw as the day's food supply for his ferrets. He gave it to them complete.

The following morning he discovered both his ferrets were dead. They had gorged themselves on the heron and died. Far better would it have been had he fed them one half of the bird one day, and the remainder on the next.

DISEASES

Regardless of how well you tend your ferrets, it is conceivable that over a period of time they will, occasionally, fall sick, however trivial the ailment might be. Thus, it is important to be able to recognise the various symptoms quickly, remove the ailing animal before the disease spreads and take appropriate action. Below are listed the ailments which are most prevalent amongst ferrets and some advice regarding their treatment.

Cuts.—Bathe with TCP solution.

Distemper.—This is identical with the distemper found in dogs. It begins with a discharge from the eyes and nose which quickly worsens. This is followed by sneezing, snuffling and shivering; eventually a cough develops. If ignored in the early stages it may turn to enteritis, vomiting, diarrhoea and finally pneumonia. If it is allowed to progress this far the chances of the ferret surviving are very slim indeed.

Treatment: once discharge is noticed, give the ferret a small amount of aspirin crushed up in fresh milk. Soluble aspirin is even better. Needless to say, the sick animal must be separated from the others and kept especially warm and dry. The eyes and nose must be kept clear by smearing with vaseline. The ferret will be disinclined to eat, but if it can be persuaded to take a little fresh meat so much the better, and it is a sign that it may be improving a little. The best diet is warm bread and milk with a little TCP added. The aspirin treatment should also be continued. Beechwood creosote sprinkled on the floor of the hutch is ideal as an inhalant, a complement to the vaseline. It is important to ensure that all sick quarters are disinfected between use.

Ear Canker.—Ear canker is caused by the same mite which infects cats and dogs, and is often contracted from this source. A common cause is the close proximity of dogs and ferrets in a vehicle en route to a day's rabbiting. It is usually fatal in young ferrets as it leads to meningitis. The symptoms are a discharge of serum and wax from the ear, and the animal becomes drowsy, losing its normal appetite.

Treatment: a mixture of 1 dr. of mercurial ointment, ½ dr. pure carbolic acid and 1 oz. of olive oil. Pour a few drops into the ears and rub well in with the fingers. Even if only one ear appears to be infected apply the treatment to both from the very beginning. Iodoform may be shaken into the ears and massaged in the same way. The treatment should be repeated every three days.

Fleas.—All ferrets pick up the odd flea from time to time, usually from rabbits in the burrow. The infected ferret should be sprayed daily with camphor or oil of sassafras, or else dusted with a flea-powder obtainable from either a pet shop or a vet. Paraffin may also be rubbed into the fur, but ensure that you are not smoking whilst administering this latter treatment! It is important to disinfect all your hutches to prevent the fleas spreading.

Hard Pad.—Hard pad as such is virtually unknown today. It is a distemper virus that was once especially prevalent in parts of Wales.

Mange.—There are two types of mange: (1) sarcoptic mange (the common type) and (2) follicular mange which is hereditary. The common variety is usually caused by a mite caught from dogs and is first noticed on the feet and around the claws.

Treatment: gammexane dressing. The infected animal should be kept warm and given ample fresh meat and milk. Sulphur ointment can also be used which is made up from sulphur, coal, tar and vegetable oil. The hutch must be disinfected to prevent the mange from spreading.

Ticks.—Ticks are blood-sucking parasites which must not be removed forcibly. Often the old warreners plucked them out with tweezers or burned them with a lighted cigarette. Much cruelty and suffering resulted and often infection followed. A little paraffin applied with a soft cloth will deal with ticks effectively. All hutches must be disinfected.

Worms.—Like fleas, worms are prevalent in ferrets, and although some discomfort is caused no serious harm will befall the animals. Nevertheless, treatment should be commenced as soon as the worms are noticed.

Treatment: mix a few grains of powdered areca nut in milk and give it to the ailing animal on an empty stomach, followed by a few drops of castor-oil.

The treatments listed for the various diseases are given as a guide to the amateur, but it would be advisable, particularly with the more serious ones, to consult a more experienced friend or a vet. The small cost of fees involved is well worth the life of a good ferret, and invariably early treatment will prove much cheaper.

BREEDING

The object in breeding from your ferrets is not only to increase your number of working animals and to provide replacements for your current ones in the future (the average life of a ferret is about five years), but to produce an even better strain.

Crossing

Consequently, it is advisable to introduce new blood by crossing your own strain with those of other owners to your mutual advantage. In order to maintain good stock, though, white and polecat ferrets should be bred separately.

There is an old belief that a jill which is not mated will die, but there is ample evidence of maiden jills having reached their normal span of life.

Mating

Once your jill comes into season arrangements should be made for a hob to be brought to her as soon as possible, the earlier the better. It is preferable for the mating to take place in *her* quarters as she is inclined to become unco-operative if taken elsewhere. The hob, apparently, has no preference for surroundings, and is only interested in the female.

The jill and the hob should be left together, *undisturbed,* for at least twenty-four hours. There will be constant squeals and scuffles, but do not be tempted to open the hutch to see what is going on for they are almost always exceedingly rough with each other.

The jill should be placed with the hob twice, on alternate days, and kept strictly apart for the rest of the time. Usually she will come on heat between March and May, but you will not know if she is pregnant until four weeks after the mating.

The period of gestation is six weeks, and during this time exercise is essential for the pregnant jill. She can safely be worked up until two weeks before giving birth, but during this last fortnight she must be confined to the breeding hutch and left well alone. Indeed, there must be no human interference until the young are fully a month old, and all cleaning-out must be suspended during this time.

CARE OF YOUNG FERRETS

The young ferrets must be fed twice daily on warm bread and milk, and also given some fresh milk. There must also be plenty of milk available for the jill.

The young will attain sight at six weeks and at eight weeks they will feed with their mother. The following month, though, is the most crucial of their lives, for it is during this time that they run the greatest risk of distemper.

If they are still healthy at ten weeks you can breathe a temporary sigh of relief, and transfer them to a separate hutch. However, they must be fed at least three times a day, applying all the feeding rules applicable to fully-grown ferrets, avoiding stale food left lying in the hutch and maintaining a constant supply of fresh water.

At twelve weeks ailments are likely to materialise, mostly of a fairly minor nature, and any sick must be moved to separate quarters. Another fortnight and if all is well they can be treated as adults.

Early handling

Early handling is essential if one is to produce good working ferrets. The more they are handled, and come to recognise the voice and scent of their owner, the better. However, one must not commence regular handling until at least ten weeks otherwise the jill may kill them.

With regard to handling, there must be no hesitancy on the part of the handler. Ferrets, like most other animals, can detect fear in a human being, and will react accordingly. One must approach them slowly with the fingers of the hand outstretched above their heads, and pick them up by the neck.

It is a mistake to commence handling by wearing gloves. It will merely mask the scent and feel of your hand, and the first time that you attempt to pick them up with an ungloved hand you will more than likely receive a bite which will keep you awake for several nights, a dull throbbing which is far worse than any bout of toothache.

Talk to your ferrets so that they become used to the sound of your voice, but never shout at them, no matter how angry you are with them. You cannot reprimand or punish them in the same way as a dog. They will either co-operate or else they won't. And in nine cases out of ten failure will be the fault of the owner. Constant coaxing is the key to success.

Plenty of vision for shooting so a good target Photo: Lance Smith

CHAPTER 3

The Quarry

Before we discuss either the training or the working of ferrets, it is essential that we fully understand the quarry which we shall pursue. Some knowledge of the ways of both the rabbit and the rat are necessary if we are to hunt them successfully.

THE RABBIT

The rabbit is ubiquitous, and after several years of absence—due to the outbreak of myxomatosis in 1953 (which we shall look at in detail later)—it is now coming back strong in both rural and urban areas. Most railway embankments in the heart of large cities have their own coney population.

The rabbit is a prolific breeder, the doe producing at least a couple of litters of nine young between March and September. These, in turn, are ready to breed at six months, so this gives us some idea of the rate at which this species is capable of multiplying. They have many enemies—including foxes, badgers, birds of prey and all members of the weasel tribe—which is possibly just as well, otherwise growing crops would be decimated on a nationwide scale.

Feeding

Rabbits feed mainly in the early morning and late evening, and sometimes in mild dry weather they will stop out all night. They present a serious threat to forestry in so much that they are very partial to the bark of young trees and sometimes do immense damage to newly planted woods.

Danger from Wounded Rabbits

Their warrens are to be found almost anywhere, sometimes in the midst of dense undergrowth where even the man from the Ministry cannot get at them with his tin of gas. However, the rabbit is not the coward which he is fondly supposed to be, his main weapon of defence being a pair of exceedingly powerful back legs which are capable of inflicting injury to man or beast of prey. Care should always be taken when picking up a wounded rabbit. If you grab one back leg only, the other is likely to inflict a painful scratch on your hand. The best method is to hold both tightly together, and a sharp downwards chop with the free hand will break the neck instantly. Alternatively, you can stretch the neck until you hear it crack.

Occasionally, the rabbit will bite, but usually this happens when one attempts to pull it from the burrow and the fumbling fingers are in contact with the animal's head.

The greatest catastrophe in the history of the rabbit is myxomatosis, and it is advisable for every true sportsman to be familiar with the ravages of this vile disease. Although rabbits have now developed immunity to some extent, there are still isolated outbreaks in various parts of the country from time to time. Doubtless many of these are deliberately spread by ruthless persons with no regard for the suffering which they cause, and it is up to us, the present generation of sportsmen, to report any such instances which come to our notice. Provided that the necessary proof can be produced, the culprits will face prosecution.

Myxomatosis

One farmer, who has just completed his harvest expressed surprise at the number of rabbits which had bolted from his barley fields. Apparently, only as recently as May, the rabbits on his 500-acre farm had contracted myxomatosis, and when the hay was mown very few conies were seen at all. How was it that they could have made such a complete recovery in so short a time?

This is not the first time that this question has been raised. Are rabbits now partially immune from this dreaded scourge, and can Nature effect a complete cure within a matter of weeks?

Of course, there is no complete answer to this. When myxomatosis was first introduced into this country way back in 1953, devastation was widespread apart from a few isolated warrens which were responsible for keeping the species going. The disease is carried by fleas, and unless infected rabbits come into contact with others, then the scourge will be contained.

Illegal Spreading of the Disease.—It is no secret that myxomatosis is spread deliberately by some ruthless farmers and landowners, and even the heavy penalties which they face if they are caught does not seem to deter them. The risk of discovery is minimal. A coney with myxomatosis is easily caught alive, and it is no difficult task to transport it to a place where healthy ones exist. Once that rabbit is introduced into the warrens, an outbreak of myxomatosis can be expected within a very short time. A neighbouring farmer can reduce an adjacent rabbit population with

This myxomatosis rabbit sought final refuge in a suburban garden

the greatest of ease. It is rumoured that high prices are being asked for infected rabbits and those who deal in this vile trade can expect little public sympathy if their activities are exposed.

So, we can assume that in many cases an outbreak of myxomatosis has been purposely spread, and he who owns the particular land is usually in total ignorance regarding its origin. Fortunately, though, the disease is not the killer it was. Mainly, this is due to the fact that a good many rabbits have now changed their habits, spending more time above ground in rough cover. The warmth and crowded burrows of an underground colony, where the fleas will travel from one coney to another, is no longer the breeding ground of myxomatosis. Mating is when rabbits come into closest contact, and although this happens from February to September, May is possibly the time when myxomatosis will spread widely. After their early spring matings, the rabbits will fall victims to the scourge about May, hence this farmer previously mentioned noticed the absence of his resident colony.

Immunity.—Rabbits are affected individually by myxomatosis in the same way that a disease amongst humans destroys the weak and ailing. The one that you see hopping slowly about, blind and insensitive to your presence, will not recover. Yet, its more healthy companion will show little more than a slight swelling around the eyes which will clear up in a matter of a week or so. There is a certain amount of immunity amongst rabbits concerning this terrible disease, but only the strongest will survive, say 20 per cent.

On 500 acres of land there may be three separate rabbit warrens. In one of these—where the inhabitants are prone to spend more of their time underground than the other two, possibly due to a location which offers little in the way of cover above ground—myxomatosis will be rife. The farmer will see the diseased conies skulking in the hedgerows and will assume that all his rabbits have contracted myxomatosis. A foray with guns and dogs after the infected rabbits is the only way to prevent it spreading further.

However, spring arrives, the healthy rabbits breed prolifically, and the most common fallacy of all is that those with myxomatosis have made some sort of miraculous recovery. It *is* a fallacy. Those unfortunates are dead and gone. A more healthy colony has taken over their warrens, and for a time all is well.

Strangely, myxomatosis is more prevalent during times of cold weather. This is because the conies are forced underground, seeking the warmth of each others' bodies, and the fleas run freely from one to another. The best antidote is a long dry summer. The rabbits can live above ground for weeks at a time, and possibly the disease would disappear altogether if it was not for human intervention.

Victory for the Rabbit.—Yet, the rabbit has definitely won through after more than twenty years of frequent outbreaks of myxomatosis. Gradually, their numbers have increased and re-established themselves. There is little danger of a widespread epidemic again on the 1953 scale. Small colonies will be wiped out, but others will take their place.

The rabbit is back, and this time he is going to stay!

Rabbits in Isolation.—The following account will further substantiate our findings concerning myxamatosis. In various parts of the British Isles there are places so desolate that a rabbit population will either be wiped out completely by the disease or else escape it altogether. Yet, it is these same rabbits which pay the penalty for inter-breeding. No fresh blood is introduced into a particular strain, and in due course this must take its toll. Nature herself, then, intervenes, reduces the existing colonies and allows them to begin breeding all over again.

"RABBIT VALLEY"

Tucked away in a remote corner of south-west Scotland is a small valley so cut off from the rest of the civilised world that it is hard to believe that the thriving county seat of Dumfries is only a short distance away. Access to Manquhill (pronounced "Manwill") is by means of a narrow rutted track through two separate hill farms, finally terminating in a cul-de-sac with heather covered hillsides towering above. Here, the shepherd fights a lone battle with the elements, his thick-walled white-washed cottage in stark contrast to the rolling background.

On one of the steep slopes there is a thicket of Scots' pines, comprising some five or six acres, still in their infancy, yet providing warm shelter for the hardy mountain sheep. Apart from this, there is nothing except grass and heather. The rocky peaks above tempt one to climb in the hope of a panoramic view of this intriguing landscape, but when we finally reach them, we discover another jagged range beyond them. After still greater efforts, we attain our goal, and find that we are standing on a flat plateau of moorland. Below us lies Manquhill, the shepherd's cottage seemingly a doll's house half hidden in the deep heather below.

The moor stretches on until it joins with another incline, and still more mountains, a treacherous place of hidden bogs and precipices, a trap for the unwary, or the stranger, should low cloud chance to drift across, obliterating all landmarks.

Yet, one has only to walk a few yards on to the Manquhill Moor before rabbits are jumping up from the tussocks of grass and heather. A few yards further on they disappear down one of the many holes in which one must take care not to step, and perhaps twist or break an ankle.

Rabbits Grazing a Grouse Moor

It is soon apparent that this is no isolated warren of conies. The whole moor, some two thousand acres, is alive with rabbits. Grouse and blackgame, where it would be reasonable to expect to find them, are surprisingly few and far between, those that rise being well out of gunshot in the manner of a well-driven moor as the season progresses. However, Manquhill is shot sparingly, and the only conclusion one can draw is that the rabbits, thriving here as they did elsewhere in pre-myxomatosis days, have grazed those tender young heather shoots which provide the birds with their staple diet.

The Curse of Inter-breeding

The Manquhill rabbits in their isolated outpost survived the worst of the myxomatosis plague, yet their curse was in their own inter-breeding. Their years of survival were blighted by liver and kidney diseases discovered only in the skinning of shot rabbits. Foxes and buzzards doubtlessly effectively cleared those that died on the moor.

Such was the case up until October 1975 when the author returned there after an absence of a couple of years, to shoot with a couple of friends. Grouse would be a bonus, and they fully expected to drive away with a car load of conies, something which they had never failed to achieve in previous years.

Within a matter of minutes the expected rabbits were bolting from cover at their approach. Seven fell to the guns in the first ten minutes, and it was only then that the terrible realisation dawned upon the shooters. Five of those seven were in an advanced stage of myxomatosis! Manquhill, the once impregnable last stronghold of the rabbit, had finally been breached.

The remainder of that day was, in effect, a mission of mercy on the part of the guns. Occasionally, they bowled over a healthy coney which was transferred to the game-bag with an eagerness hitherto foreign to all shooting men in this lost valley, but mostly the corpses were disposed of in the sucking bogs.

Recovery from Myxomatosis?

Yet, the rabbits of Manquhill will rise once again. No country-lover welcomes the ugly reappearance of this terrible disease, bringing with it a lingering death to the unfortunate victims, but, in this instance, perhaps Nature herself has decreed that it is the only way in which a healthy stock can be re-introduced. The law of the wild is the survival of the fittest, and this was brought home to the writer as the shadows lengthened over the hills, and he bowled over the last rabbit of the day as the party trudged back downhill towards the parked vehicle.

The only too familiar horrific markings were apparent around the eyes of the dead creature, yet instead of the usual matter-filled swellings they resembled peeling scars. Although no expert in the forms this vile disease takes, the author is convinced that the rabbit in question had overcome its crisis, and was on the road to recovery, and *immunity.*

There is another factor which is instrumental, to a

lesser degree, in reducing the rabbit populations of our countryside, and it is worthwhile taking a brief look at this if only for the conclusions which we are able to draw from this exercise.

Rabbits Killed on the Roads

On a recent journey through Lincolnshire and Norfolk, during the month of August, the author was astounded at the number of rabbits which had been killed on the roads. Between Bourne and Spalding, he counted in the region of forty conies which had met their end beneath the wheels of speeding motor-vehicles, and possibly another twenty in the short distance between Hunstanton and Brancaster. It was mostly just in these two particular areas that the majority of the deaths had taken place, and although he covered something like 150 miles of roads in these two eastern counties, he only came across the odd dead rabbit elsewhere. Not one dead hare was seen during the whole journey!

Increasing Rabbit Population

These rough statistics give much food for thought. The first thing that springs to mind, obviously, is that both areas mentioned have a rapidly increasing rabbit population. Two-thirds of those killed were little more than half-grown, and whilst this illustrates their inexperience in crossing busy roads, it also means that the rabbits in these localities are breeding prolifically. In many ways, one is saddened by this wanton killing, whilst fully realising, at the same time, that drivers must not risk human life by swerving to avoid a rabbit which sits in the road, mesmerised by oncoming headlights. Some motorists deliberately run over rabbits, either hoping to acquire a cheap meal, if they do not damage it too badly, but mainly because they simply cannot resist "having a go".

Rabbits today are living more above ground than they did in pre-myxomatosis days. This means that they have no "permanent" homes in the form of warrens, and are, consequently, much more prone to move from field to field, mostly during the hours of darkness. Hence, more rabbits are crossing roads, and as the number of motorists is increasing daily, it is only to be concluded that many more coneys will be killed by cars than ever before.

Rabbit road-deaths do help, in a small way, to keep these creatures, so destructive to agriculture, under control. It may seem a waste, but, from a rabbit's point of view, a quick death beneath the wheels of a car is preferable to dying slowly from disease brought about by over-population.

Rabbits in Lincolnshire are more prone to be "nomads" than in any other county in the British Isles. The absence of hedges and large tracts of woodlands, means that they have to survive in amongst growing crops which will, eventually, be harvested, depriving them of their protective cover. They may be forced to move from a field of barley into a field of potatoes once harvesting starts, and then, before long, they are disturbed again. This time they may take up residence in either cabbages, rape or sugar-beet. There is no rest for them.

The fact that there was not a single hare amongst the slain is remarkable in itself. There is an old theory that rabbits and hares will not live in the same area because the buck rabbit goes out of his way to kill the young leverets. There may be a certain element of truth in this, but I would be inclined to think that, in a county such as Lincolnshire, where woods are not so dense as in other parts of the country, the two species would have to live fairly close together if they were to

A hare on the alert, perhaps fearing the attack of a buck rabbit on her leverets

The Brown Rat—A destructive creature

obtain any sort of cover from crop rotation. Even if they are not prepared to integrate, then they will have to tolerate each other as neighbours.

Why, then, were there no hares amongst the rabbits killed on the roads that particular day? First, the rabbits outnumber the larger animal by far, and so, on the law of averages, more must be killed. However, my own theory is that the female hare makes a far better mother than does her rabbit counterpart. She will do her best to keep her young away from busy roads, probably in the centre of a large cornfield where they can play, feed and enjoy maximum safety. They are content to remain in one field for weeks on end, whereas the rabbit is a compulsive wanderer.

It is reasonably safe to assume that the humble coney will be with us for a long time to come, and this should gladden the hearts of most sportsmen.

Yet, the other quarry which the ferreter may pursue presents a totally different picture in our countryside. I have yet to meet anyone who claims to have any form of affection for the rat.

THE RAT

The brown rat begins to breed when it is six months old, producing four or five litters a year with from four to ten in each. On average, then, one female rat is capable of multiplying fifty times per annum. Even the rabbit cannot equal this. The rat, though, is a much more vicious creature, destructive to livestock, crops and property, as well as adding to its obnoxious presence by the spreading of disease.

Of course, there are more effective methods of rat-control then ferreting. Poison laid by an official rodent-operator is probably the best, yet there is no reason why we should not take advantage of some sport at the expense of this filthy species.

Where rats are concerned one can only generalise. They are to be found almost anywhere, in fields, woods, the banks of streams and rivers (not to be confused with water-voles), outbuildings, old houses, and virtually in any locality where there is food to scavenge.

The rat is a dangerous enemy, and must be killed whenever the opportunity presents itself.

Rabbits present a difficult target in thick gorse Photo: Lance Smith

Entering the ferret Photo: David Cluett
Also see Page 69

CHAPTER 4

Training and Working Ferrets to Rabbits and Rats

Needless to say, one cannot breed ferrets and, as soon as they are twelve weeks old, take them out on a major rabbiting or ratting expedition. In the case of the latter, possibly 75 per cent of the ferrets would be killed by an adversary against which they were powerless to defend themselves. Likewise, untrained, they would probably become lost in a large rabbit burrow, and we should be lucky to recover them all even by digging out.

IMPORTANCE OF HANDLING

Early handling is the most important feature of training. Ferrets must become used to their owner, to his touch, and to the sound of his voice. Both must be confident. A shy owner is as bad as a shy ferret.

Pick up your ferret in the manner already described, but do not hold it too tightly. A crushing grip is liable to frighten the creature, and in all probability it will bite you. You must always show kindness, but at the same time remain the boss. The sooner you win the respect and confidence of your ferret, the sooner you will be able to make a start in earnest on the warrens.

START WITH A HOLE IN A BANK

Young ferrets are always keener to enter holes which

slope *upwards* than one which disappears into the bowels of the earth so if you can find a suitable bank where there are rabbits then this will be ideal.

It is important to find a rabbit on the first outing otherwise your young ferrets may become bored with the apparently useless exercise of exploring empty holes. So take the mother and a couple of young ferrets to a burrow where there is a good chance of discovering a rabbit. Use a line on the jill and allow the youngsters to accompany her into the warren.

It is a good idea whenever you use "a liner" to tie small pieces of ribbon at intervals of a yard along the line. In this way you will have a good idea of how far the ferret has travelled underground.

YOUNG FERRETS BENEFIT FROM BEING DUG OUT

The jill enters the most likely looking entrance and the youngsters follow her. There is always the possibility that she may move a rabbit and that the young ferrets will kill it. In all probability, in this case, they will have to be dug out, but they will benefit from the lesson. Ferrets do not like being removed in this way, and the sooner that they learn that every time they lie-up they will be dug out, the more reluctant they will be to remain below ground with a rabbit they have killed. They also have a habit of wandering about aimlessly in burrows, reluctant to show themselves.

For the purpose of this book we will assume that the youngsters have killed a rabbit and lain up with it. You have retrieved the jill but had to dig out two very surprised youngsters. That will do for today. Do not try another hole. They have experienced what rabbiting is all about so let them dwell on this. Return them to the hutch and if possible set out again on the

Return this ferret to a *different* hole

morrow.

Use a Deserted Warren for the Second Lesson

The second lesson should be in a warren where there is little chance of finding a rabbit. Take the jill along, again on a line, and proceed as before. You should now be able to note a certain amount of keenness in your young ferrets. They remember the last outing, and now they will work eagerly in the hope of finding another rabbit.

After some time, their search being fruitless, they will emerge into the open. You must return them to the burrow by *a different hole* at once. They are inclined to become bored with the whole proceedings if the same hole is used a second time.

Avoid Boredom

Do not prolong this lesson for more than an hour. As in the case of training a puppy, boredom must be avoided. Even inexperienced ferrets will realise after a time that there are no rabbits in the burrow and the last thing you want is to have them frolicking about below ground.

It depends upon the intelligence of your ferrets how many lessons will be needed before they are ready for the real thing. Some need no more than a couple, others three or four. Rarely does one come across a young ferret which is absolutely useless. Like humans, some take longer to learn than others.

The main points to look for are keenness in your ferrets, and a willingness to return to hand without hesitation. Once these are apparent your battle is half won.

Never allow young ferrets to remain below ground for more than about twenty minutes. If they have not shown up by then it is a fair assumption that they are intent upon lying-up. Dig them out!

Net Rabbits During Training Sessions

During these training sessions rabbits should be netted rather than shot. Do not confuse or frighten your ferrets with gunfire. Allow them to concentrate fully on the business of bolting rabbits.

Dogs, too, should be left at home. The two must be introduced to each other gradually, and a training session is not the time to begin an acquaintance between dog and ferret.

The best way of getting your dog and ferrets used to each other is by allowing the former to accompany you whilst you feed and clean-out the latter. Rarely do either take a dislike to each other after the first meeting.

Training for Rats

There is no difference between training ferrets for rabbits and training them for rats. It is probably easier, though, to begin by teaching them to enter rabbit warrens, because if they decide to lie up in a rat-hole beneath a barn or out-building, retrieving them will not be an easy task.

The main thing to bear in mind, though, is that there is no similarity between the rabbit and the rat. The rat is a vicious fierce fighter, and your ferret will become involved in many a battle. **Therefore, only use fully-trained ferrets for ratting.**

EQUIPMENT

Before we embark upon an assault of the warrens we must consider the equipment necessary to make our task that much more efficient and easy.

The following items are basic equipment which every ferreter should possess:

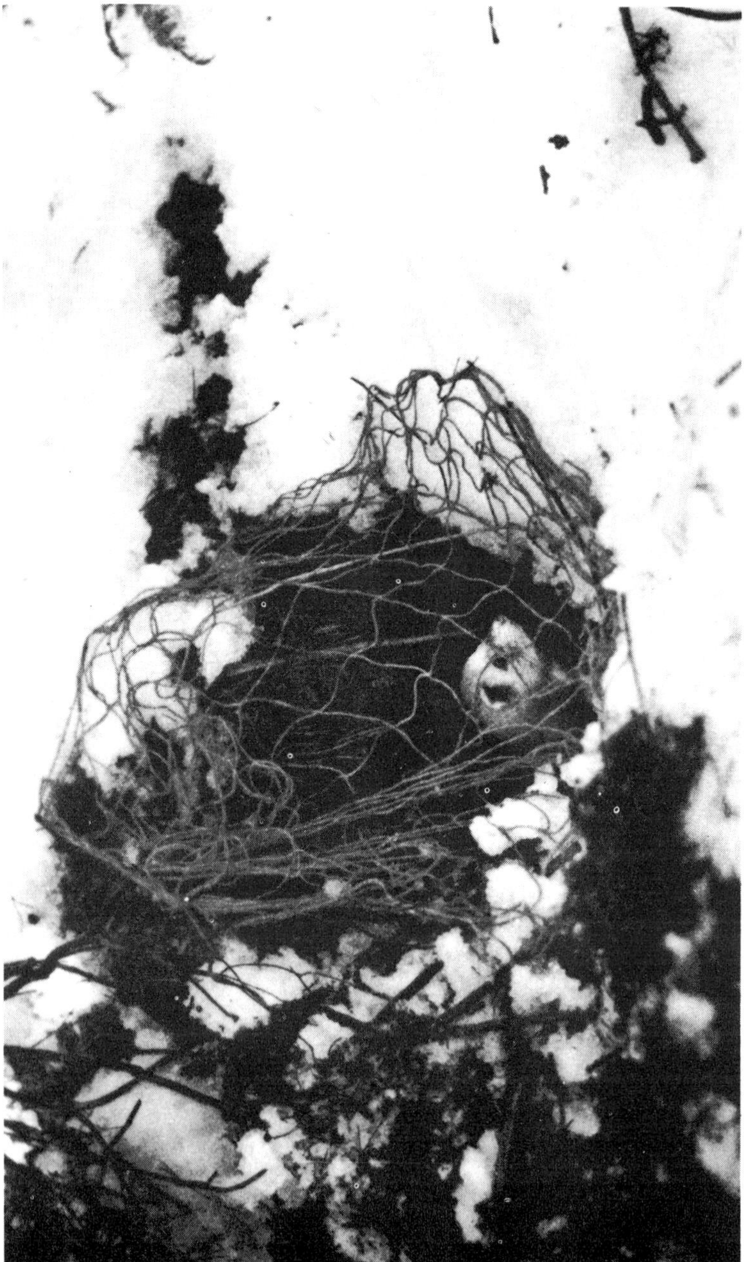

Boredom must be avoided. This ferret shows a lack of interest having explored a deserted warren

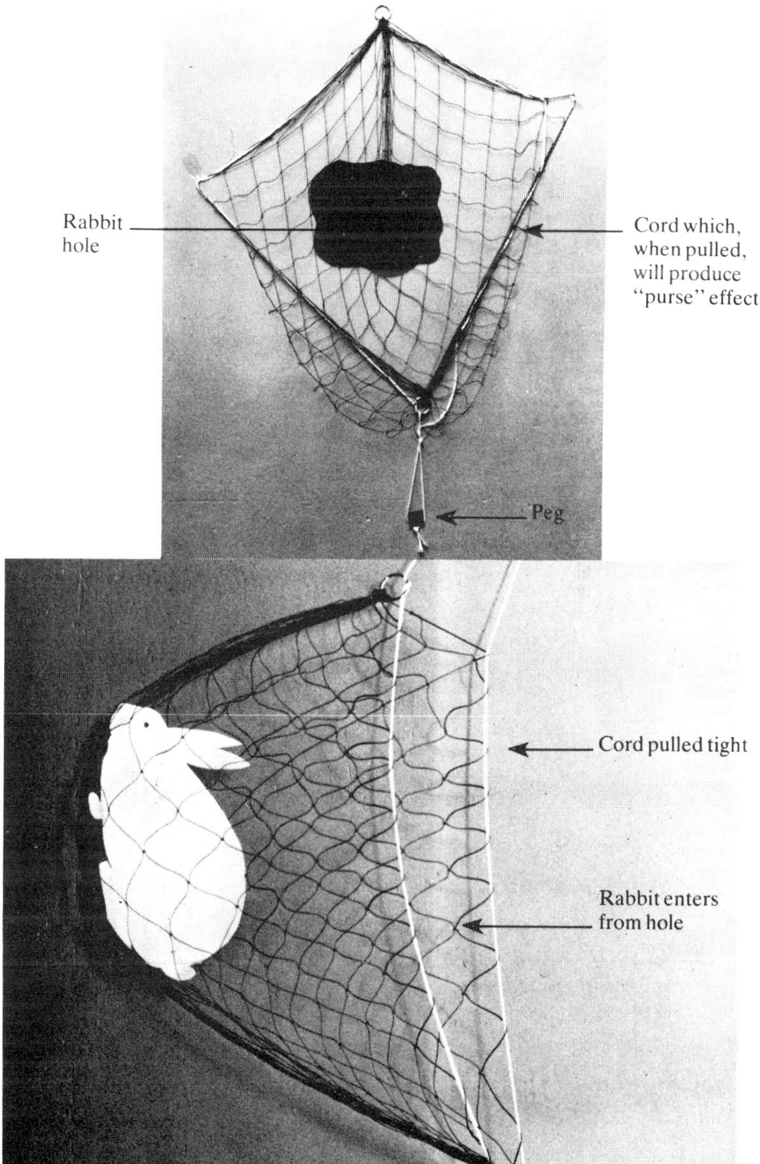

Top: Net opened to simulate positioning over hole
Bottom: Net showing "purse" effect when rabbit is trapped

2. Placing net over hole

3. Inserting ferret into hole

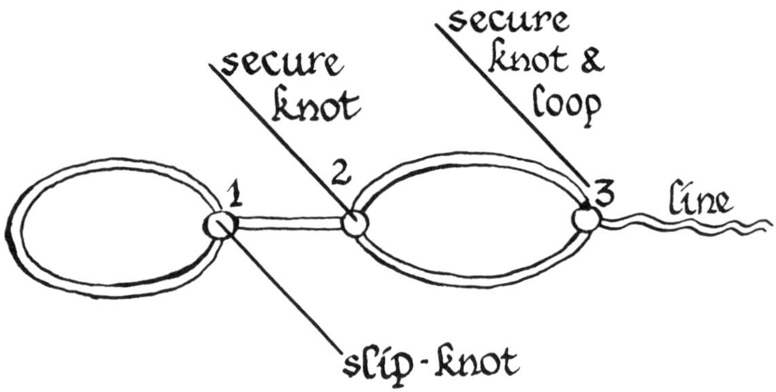

AN EASY-TO-MAKE MUZZLE

The first loop goes over the ferret's muzzle and is fastened by the slip knot (1). The second loop goes around the ferret's neck. Knots 2 and 3 must be secure, and not slip knots otherwise there is a danger of strangling the ferret.

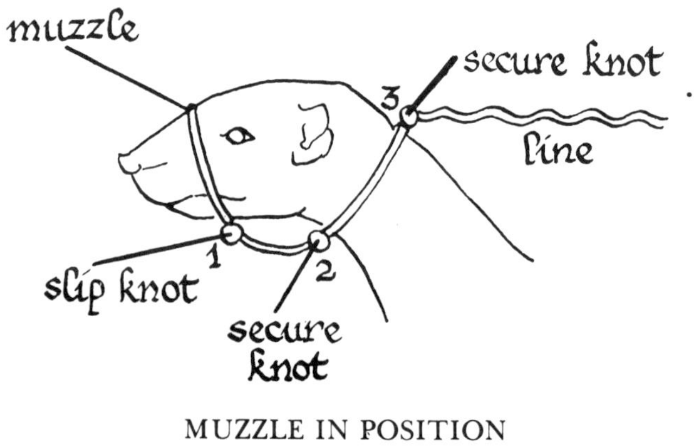

MUZZLE IN POSITION

(1) **Muzzles**—I do not advocate the use of muzzles except in the case of an adult jill during training or when attempting to move youngsters which have lain up with a kill. My main objection to a muzzle is that a lost ferret is liable to starve if not recovered within two or three days.
(2) **A rod** for probing burrows in an attempt to locate a missing ferret. One of the collapsible aluminium variety is light and convenient to carry.
(3) **A spade** for that occasion when you will be forced to dig your ferret out.
(4) **Purse-nets**—the number you will need will depend upon the size of the warrens you intend to tackle. These can be transported easily if you fold them and tie them to their individual pegs. In this way they will not become entangled with each other, and can be made ready for use in a matter of seconds.
(5) **Knee-caps**—leather knee-caps are an investment against rheumatism in later life. Mostly during the winter months, when ferreting is at its height, you will be kneeling on wet, frosty and snow-covered ground.
(6) **Carrying-box**—a box is better for transporting ferrets than a bag. The ferrets are much more comfortable as they have room to move about, and a bag is always liable to become saturated if it rains. Likewise, in a bag ferrets can be trodden on or worried by a dog not able to see what it contains.
(7) **A hammer** for driving in pegs for purse-nets.

PREPARATION FOR RABBITING

Inspect the Ground

It is no good arranging a day's rabbiting and then

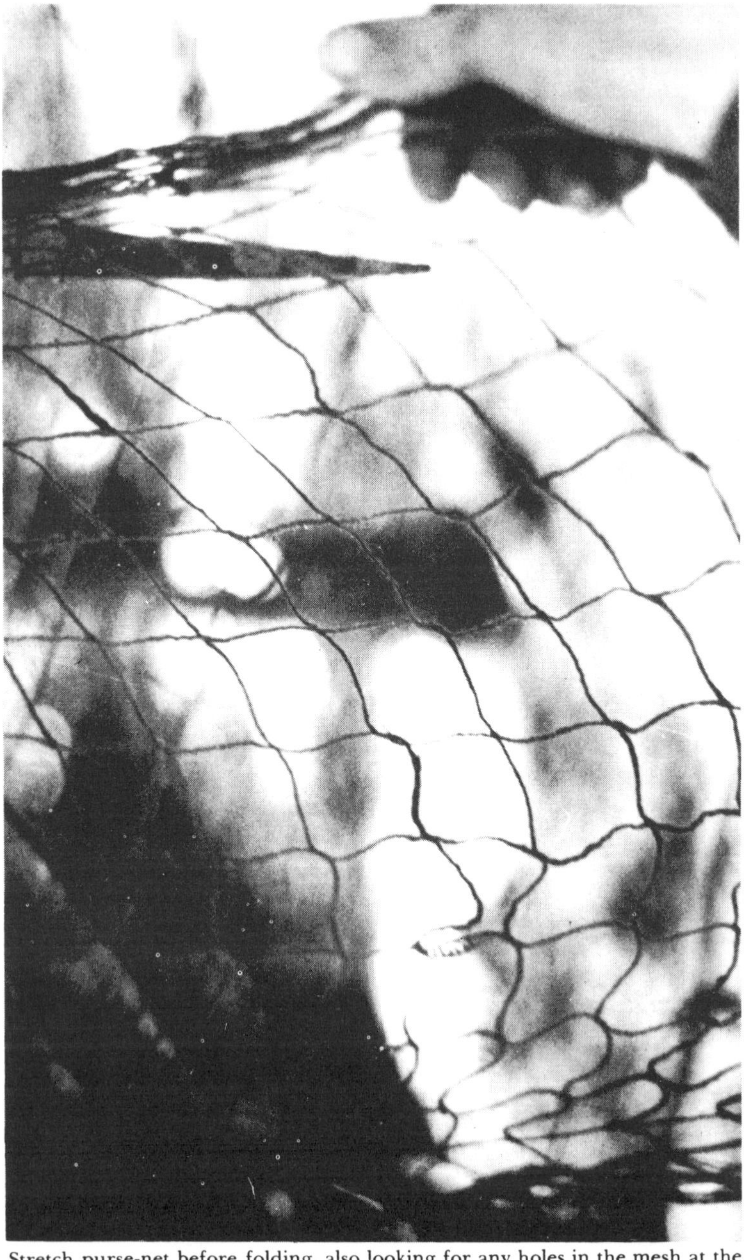

Stretch purse-net before folding, also looking for any holes in the mesh at the same time

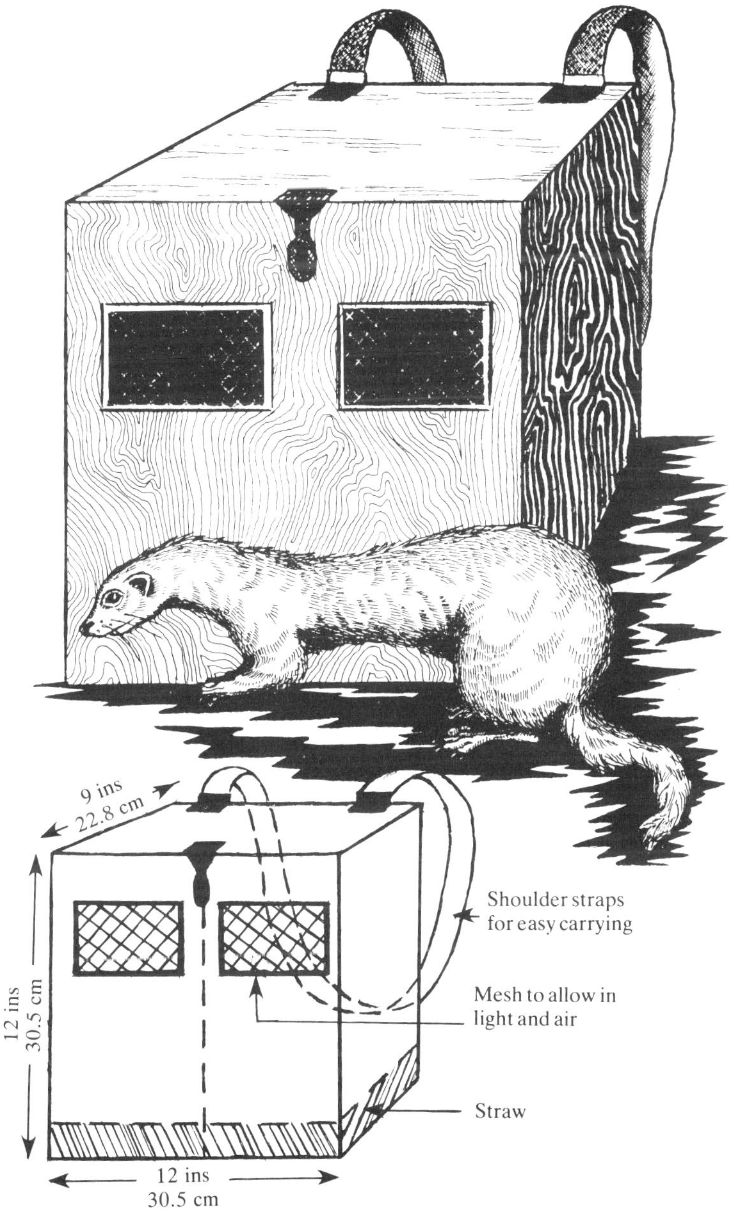

An ideal carrying box with separate compartments

leaving all preparations until the day in question. If you do that then you most certainly will have a poor day's sport.

The ground should be inspected a few days beforehand, and a search made for all entrances to the burrows which you intend to work. Sometimes it is necessary to clear brushwood and undergrowth in order to get at them. Not only would this waste time on the actual day, but the noise involved would be so great that the rabbits would be reluctant to bolt, relying on evading your ferrets below ground.

Block up Difficult Holes

Some holes present problems, especially when it is your intention to shoot the bolting rabbits. It is these that must be blocked up firmly with sods of earth in such a manner that they cannot be scratched out again before the day's sport commences, leaving only the best holes open.

Safety is Paramount

You must plan where the guns will stand, not only with a view to obtaining the maximum amount of sport, but also with safety in mind. Where possible all the guns must be able to see each other, or if this is not possible then they must be fully aware of everyone else's position. Once a gun has been instructed to stand in a certain place then he must remain there even if it is obvious that a move of twenty yards or so would mean better shooting.

Of course, nothing ever goes exactly as you plan it. You will nearly always find that you have overlooked a hole in a clump of briars, and that one or two rabbits have gained safety before you are aware of it. Nevertheless, a reconnaissance is essential if only to give you some idea of the number of ferrets which you will need on the day.

Before we come to the "Big Day" it might be beneficial to look back upon the warrener of yesteryear, the man already mentioned in this book, who earned his living by rabbiting in a variety of ways. Whilst it is not our intention to emulate him (indeed, some of his methods are now illegal), a basic knowledge of the way in which he worked can only be helpful to the novice. One point must be borne in mind, though. The professional rabbit-catcher was not concerned with sport. All that mattered to him was the number of rabbits in the bag at the end of the day. It was his livelihood.

THE OLD RABBIT-CATCHERS

The rabbit-catchers are only just a memory to most of us. Indeed, it seems a far cry to those days when wild rabbits could be seen in their hundreds. The farming fraternity demanded their control, and this, in turn, led to a breed of men who, for the period between the two wars, made their living from trap, snare and purse-net, their only companions for weeks on end being their ferrets.

Even after World War II there were still a few of these warreners left, eking a bare existence from the coney populations which were still fairly prolific throughout the British Isles. Finally, it was myxamatosis which dealt the final blow to these hardy men. The rabbits went, and so did the warreners.

TRAPPING

However, let us take a closer look at these men who systematically worked one warren after another. First, their equipment and methods. The cruel gin-trap (now illegal) was mostly used in sandy ground. The rabbit runs were easy to determine here,

Undergrowth such as this should be cleared before ferreting is attempted. There will be many otherwise unseen holes amongst it by which rabbits will bolt and escape both nets and guns and the warrener would spend the majority of the daylight hours knocking in stout stakes to which he would tether the lengthy chains. Then, he would set the gins in the runs, half burying them in the sand, lightly set so that at the slightest touch of a rabbit's foot those cruel jaws would spring into instant action.

Snaring

Snaring is carried out on much the same lines, except that the setting of these wire nooses is much more intricate. Not only must one determine which tracks are more recently used than others, but a closer examination must be carried out so that the snares can be set *between* the rabbits' jumps. Failure to do this will result in a host of snares simply being knocked over.

FERRETING IS THE MOST SPORTING METHOD OF RABBIT CONTROL

From a sporting angle, there is nothing to compare with ferreting. The man who uses purse-nets in preference to a gun will bag far more rabbits for he will be able to work silently without alarming the bolting rabbits. A calm day is essential when one will be able to hear the rabbits moving about below ground. Moving as quietly as possible, the rabbit-catcher places a purse-net over every hole in the warren. Often, one in the midst of a thorn bush or dense undergrowth will be overlooked, and several rabbits will escape by this exit. Yet, it is all in the game.

Once the nets are in position, the ferret is introduced into one of the holes. Then one must be patient. Rabbits may start to bolt at once, or it could take half an hour or more before they begin to move.

The warrener has to be quick. The moment there is a rabbit in a net, then he must pounce immediately and despatch the struggling creature with a sharp blow on the head.

MYXOMATOSIS HERALDED THE END OF THE WARRENER

Often, large numbers of rabbits were taken in one day by any of these three methods. It was a way of life which now, sadly, is gone. Even when the coney population began increasing after myxomatosis had spread its initial devastation, the warrener did not reappear. There were far easier, and more lucrative ways, in which to make a living. Rabbit control became a government responsibility, which had every vestige of romance removed from it. Cyanide gas replaced traps, snares and purse-nets. In this way a whole warren can be ruthlessly and systematically destroyed in a matter of minutes. The rabbit which used to escape the old-time rabbit-catcher by using that hidden hole in the briar bush, now has no chance. Also, in these days of rising food prices, a valuable meat supply has been wasted. Only the sporting man will provide rabbits for the table. The farmer will argue that a decline in the rabbit population means a greater harvest. Yet, were those pre-war harvests so bad when the rabbit was prolific?

CROSSING BELGIAN HARES WITH RABBITS

The author has recollections, going back many years, of the days when hundreds of rabbits were killed annually on less than a hundred acres of land close to his own home. This acreage will never see these numbers of conies again, and the reason has nothing whatsoever to do with myxomatosis, for on it now stands a television mast and transmitting station, alongside the huge craters which have been made by those who constantly quarry for sand and gravel.

It is indeed a sad sight for anyone who knew the fields and woodlands there originally. The "New Plantation Wood", admittedly, has not yet suffered from the depredations of quarrying, although the workings are within a few feet of it, but the disturbance has been enough to drive every form of wildlife well away from it.

The rabbits which lived and bred there in such numbers, both before and during the last war, were no ordinary rabbits. They were slightly larger in size, and their fur was of a bluish colour. The author can remember the days when his father rented the shooting rights there, and although the rabbiting was let separately, he was entitled to shoot all those that he put up during the normal course of walking through in search of game. He used to average between six and eight rabbits each Saturday afternoon, whilst the man who rented the ground game was snaring and ferreting four or five times this number. The quality of these particular rabbits was due to the release of a stock of Belgian hares by a previous shooting tenant during the 1930s. This creature, unlike the common brown hare, will inter-breed with wild rabbits, and hence this magnificent strain was introduced into the existing stock. Another factor which favours the introduction of this foreign strain is that the author cannot remember his father bringing home any diseased rabbits, which would only be expected in areas where these creatures have been allowed to live and breed closely amongst themselves. Nowadays, anyone caught attempting to increase a rabbit population would be severely punished by law.

It was a wonderful sight, on a spring

evening—though perhaps not to the tenant farmer—to see droves of these large, healthy rabbits playing on the edge of the woods. It is a sight which this place will never see again, for the march of progress and civilization has sealed the fate of this once excellent rabbit shoot.

RABBITING IN EARNEST

At last the Big Day arrives, and you set forth with your ferrets and equipment to the burrows, full of optimism. Conditions are ideal, a calm day when you will be able to hear the rabbits moving about below ground in the warrens.

There are three of you, including yourself. The other two are carrying guns to deal with those rabbits which escape your nets. You are the operator, the man upon whom success or failure rests.

Rabbits Usually Bolt Uphill

You have visited this tract of ground on the day before yesterday, cut back some undergrowth and blocked up a few holes in the surrounding bracken. The site in question is a large sloping wood, and this being the case you motion to your two companions to take up their respective stances *above* the big warren. Whenever possible rabbits will always try to bolt uphill and, in any case, you appear to have covered all the lower holes.

Silence is Important

You move about as quietly as you can, hammering in the pegs for your purse-nets, and trying to make as little noise as possible. Some ferreters favour a frosty morning, but the main drawback is that you will make too much noise walking about on top of the burrow akin to treading on a layer of crispy breakfast cereal.

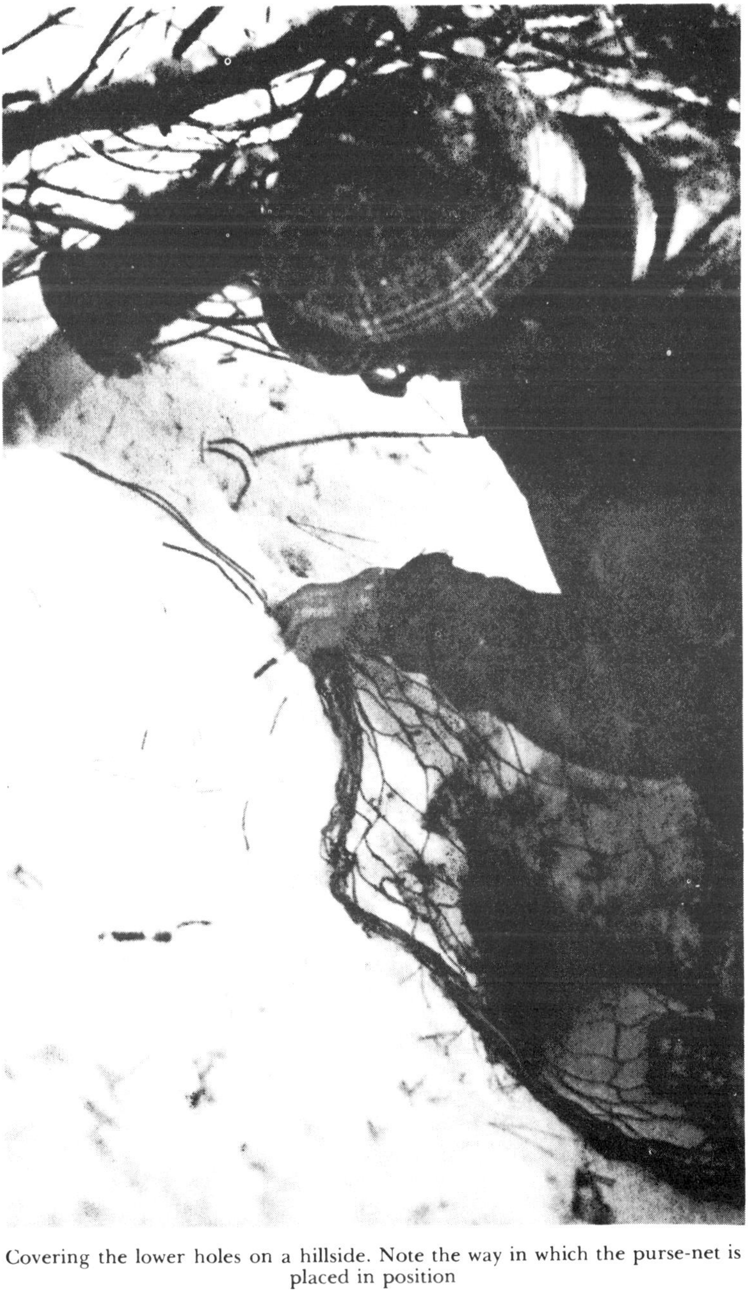

Covering the lower holes on a hillside. Note the way in which the purse-net is placed in position

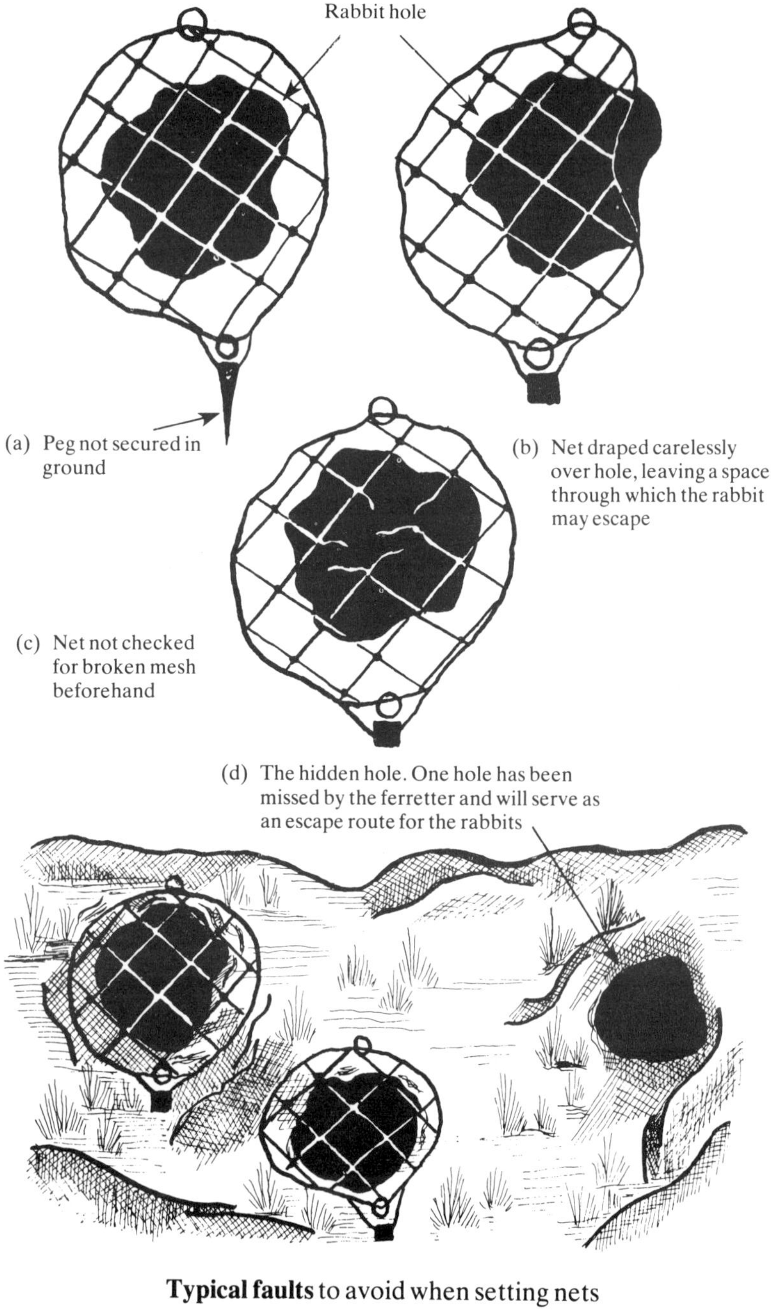

Typical faults to avoid when setting nets

Rabbits rarely bolt well in windy weather.

You have a dual purpose in mind—sport for your friends and rabbit-control for the farmer. It is your nets which should provide the majority of the bag.

All is ready, and a raised hand signals to the two guns that you are about to put a couple of ferrets into the burrow. You watch the latter disappear below ground and the excitement begins to build up inside you.

Five minutes, ten . . . . . and there is no sign of a rabbit. One of the ferrets emerges from a hole near to you so you retrieve it and put it in another entrance.

A few minutes later the crashing report of a twelve-bore shatters the stillness. One of your companions signals that he has been successful and then you are suddenly busy yourself. No sooner have you dived onto a rabbit in a net three yards to your left than another one becomes entangled in one to your right.

Three in the bag, and then all goes quiet again. You lie on the ground directly on top of the burrow, listening intently. You can hear movements below you, the thumping scamper of a rabbit going uphill and away from you. A quick double-shot, followed by a thumbs-down sign from one of your colleagues. There is always the one which gets away!

Digging-out

Twenty minutes later, with no further action, you manage to catch two of your ferrets which have shown themselves. It is fairly obvious that the third one is intent upon lying-up. With a grimace you fetch the rods and spade, and begin to probe down the burrow in which you entered your missing ferret. Approximately four yards and you meet with an obstruction. Removing your jacket you start to dig.

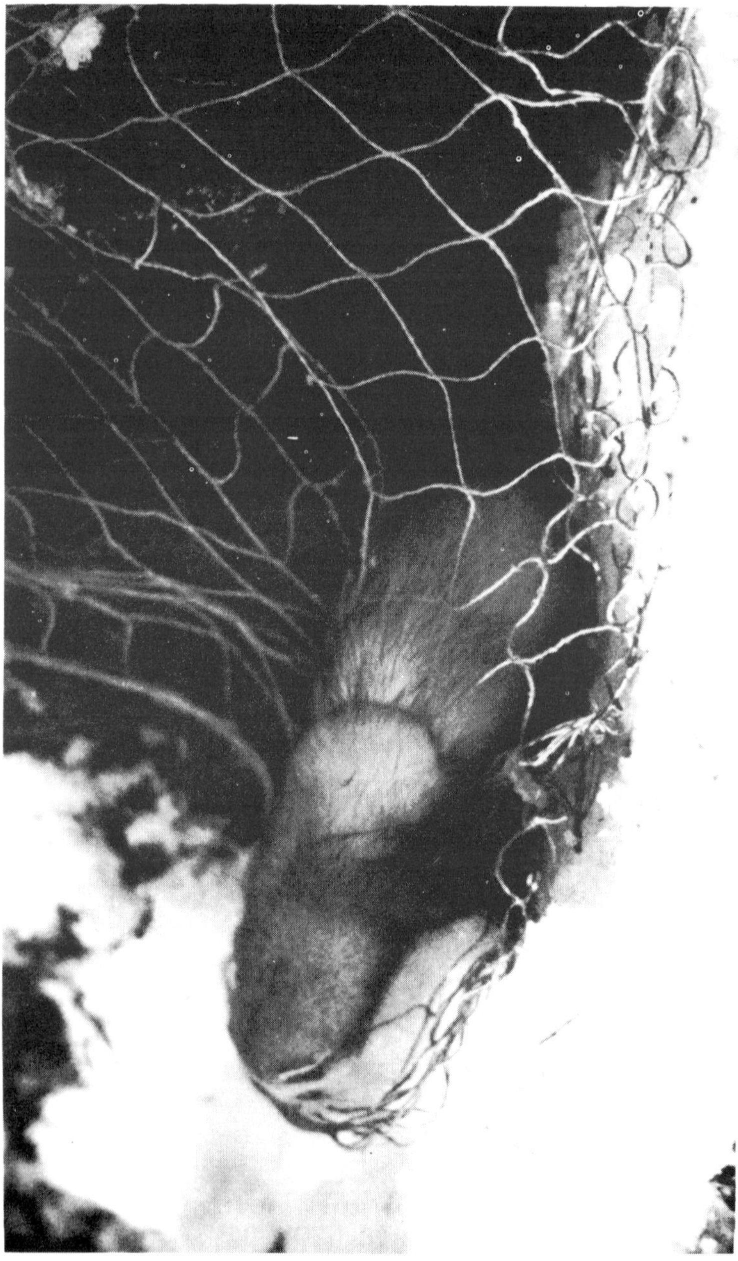

Nothing doing in this hole

After about ten minutes you come upon a dead rabbit. A yard further on you find another, but still no ferret. Another two yards and you find your ferret, lying up with a third rabbit!

Six rabbits out of that burrow, and you have every right to feel satisfied with the way things are going. One always wonders how many dead rabbits are left below ground, and very often a dig helps to add to the bag. However, it should be pointed out that too much digging will ruin a good warren, and should only be undertaken when there is no other way of retrieving your ferret.

Do Not Smoke Out a Missing Ferret

Smoke candles, or burning paper in the holes to remove a ferret, should be avoided. The author related in his book *Gamekeeping and Shooting for Amateurs* how he removed a stubborn ferret by means of discharging black gunpowder into one of the rabbit holes. That particular animal simply refused to enter a warren again.

When Your Ferret Does Not Return

There are occasions when it is impracticable to dig out a ferret that has lain up. It may well be that you are working a burrow in an old-established wood where huge roots impede your efforts with the space. Therefore, there is only one course open to you. Place some rabbit entrails in a sack, propping the neck open with a stout stick, and position it on the windward side of the hole in which your ferret disappeared. You will have to abandon the creature for the night, but return at first light, and there is every chance that you will find your ferret soundly asleep in the sack.

Every effort must be made to recover a lost ferret.

One lost ferret will constitute a danger to game and poultry in the vicinity.

Working a Burrow in a Hedge

Six rabbits in the bag, and you move on to the next burrow. This one is in the stools of a thick hawthorn hedge, and you will need to approach it more strategically. It is unlikely that all the rabbits bolted will choose the open ground on either side. Many of them will run up or down the hedgerow, so you will need to place the two guns very carefully, one on either side where they have the best view of the stools of the hedge as well as the opportunity to shoot in the open field. Each must be aware of where the other is standing.

It is not a particularly large burrow so you will need only a couple of ferrets, and there are only two holes that you can net. It is the guns who are going to have all the sport this time.

In spite of the smallness of the burrow it is a longer wait than previously, and you have almost given up hope that any rabbits will bolt when a shot rings out. Then, within the next five minutes four more conies bolt, three following the course of the hedge, and one heading across the open stubble. Two are accounted for.

Small Burrows and a Job for "the Liner"

From now onwards you will be working a succession of small burrows, mostly situated in hedgerows or overgrown corners of fields. There will be no more large ones, and here you will work a single ferret, the old jill who knows her job better than any of the others. You put her on a line, but unmuzzled, because often a single ferret under these circumstances will lie-up if it corners a rabbit in a blind alley.

Bag of rabbits after a successful afternoon's ferreting

Eventually, the late afternoon turns to dusk, and you head homewards. A dozen rabbits isn't a bad reward for your day's work.

FEED THE RABBITS' ENTRAILS TO YOUR FERRETS

Your first job on your return home is the care of your ferrets. They will be relieved to be back in the hutch after the confinement of the ferret-box, but they will be hungry.

Paunch your rabbits and feed the entrails to your ferrets. Cooked rabbit meat is always sweeter when the rabbits have been gutted within a few hours of being killed, anyway.

All that remains now is to sort out your equipment. Don't leave the untangling of your purse-nets until the time of the next foray. Sort them out now and fold them in readiness. Clean your spade, too. There is nothing more slovenly than putting away a spade caked with earth which will probably crumble and make a mess in your car on your way to the warrens next time. The carrying-box, too, will in all probability need cleaning out to prevent it from becoming foul-smelling. And, of course, there are the rabbits to be disposed of suitably. Perhaps a couple each for the guns, some in the freezer to feed the ferrets when supplies are short and, of course, some for your own table.

RABBIT RECIPES

There are many ways in which to cook a rabbit, just as, proverbially, there are alternative methods of skinning it. Most good cookery books will provide several recipes, but three of the most popular and long-standing since the days of the old warrener are:

1. *Rabbit Casserole.*—Skin and joint your rabbit. Fry the joints gently with 2 oz. of onions until the meat is lightly browned. Mix a desertspoonful of flour into the fat. Add, gradually, approximately $\frac{1}{3}$ pint of water and a glass of wine if desired. Stir, then transfer to a casserole. Add $\frac{1}{4}$ lb. mushrooms, 2 carrots and/or 2 parsnips. Cover the casserole, place in a medium oven at 375°F and cook for approximately two hours or until the meat is tender. This can also be cooked in a large saucepan on top of the cooker (*stew*).

2. *Roast Rabbit.*—One *young* rabbit, skinned, washed and dried. Stuff the rabbit with 4 oz. chopped lean ham, 8 oz. sausagemeat, 2 teaspoonfuls of chopped parsley, the grated rind of one lemon, 2 oz. of sultanas, and one egg, all mixed up. Truss. Tie fat bacon strips over the back of the rabbit and cover with

foil. Place rabbit in a roasting tin with dripping and roast in a hot oven for about an hour or until the meat is tender. Baste frequently. Sprinkle a little flour over the rabbit and return to the oven for approximately ten minutes whilst it browns. Serve with gravy made from the fat in the tin.

3. *Rabbit Pie.*—One rabbit, skinned and jointed. ½ lb. ham or bacon. One large onion, chopped up. Fry the meat and onion until it is browned in butter as in the previous recipe. Season, and add ½ pint of stock. Simmer for about three-quarters of an hour until the meat is tender. When cold, remove bones from rabbit, fill a pie-dish with meat and stock, and cover with pastry. Bake at 400°F for one hour.

Waiting for rabbits to bolt from an overgrown disused quarry
Photo: Lance Smith

A proper carrying-box provides ferrets with comfort and safety during transit. Photo: David Cluett

Also see Page 73

CHAPTER 5

Alternative Methods of Rabbit Control and Some Advice on Ratting

As we have already seen, the professional rabbit-catcher employed various ways of killing his conies. Whilst ferreting is undoubtedly the most effective and sporting, we must look at the others if we are fully to understand rabbit-control.

SNARING

Snaring is possibly the best method for the "occasional" rabbiter, the man who makes an assault on his coney population two or three times a year for which the keeping of ferrets would be superfluous. However, some knowledge and experience are necessary otherwise a great deal of time will be wasted with nothing to show for it.

A light covering of snow is ideal because one is able to see the movements of rabbits clearly, and determine the runs which are being used most frequently. Even so, a great deal more knowledge is required than simply going out and setting a few wires in these runs.

Snares are More Effective in Hedgerows, etc.

Most of the old warreners used to set their snares in the open, but where there is cover nearby, such as a thick hedgerow or a wood, the amateur will probably achieve better overall success than attempting to set his snares so precisely between the places where rabbits jump. The aim is to catch the rabbit around the neck at all times, and failure to do this results in suffering for the animal. A rabbit has considerable strength and sometimes manages to snap a wire. The last thing we want to do is to have rabbits suffering a lingering death with a snare biting through fur and flesh, and unless you judge the exact position of the head of the hopping rabbit that is what will happen. So, in the early stages concentrate on runs through hedges, gaps in fences and in woodland. In doing this you will be saved the trouble of carrying loads of pegs and a mallet, for you will have a far firmer support in fence or hedge to attach your snares.

Bury New Snares

New snares do not catch well until they have "weathered". In order to save yourself the time of having to inspect rows of bright and shiny snares, bury them in the ground for a few days.

It is always best to use a pair of thin gloves when setting, for the scent of your fingers will remain on the snares if set with bare hands.

Finding Well-used Runs

It is usually easy enough for even the rawest amateur to determine which gaps in fences or hedges are being used by rabbits. The runs will often be only too obvious, but a fall of snow will show you which are old unused ones and which are currently being travelled by your quarry on their trips to and from their burrows to feed in the fields.

Setting Snares

Set the loop of the snare about 3½ in. from the

ground, and held in position in the cleft of a small forked stick. Do not have the loop too wide or else there is a likelihood of it running over the rabbit and catching it around the middle. Snares which you find knocked down mean that you are setting them incorrectly, usually too low.

Inspect After Dark

The best time to set your snares is during the afternoon, and if you really want to make the best of your time and trouble, then inspect them about a couple of hours after dark by torchlight. Any catches can be removed before they are discovered by foxes or other vermin, and the snares reset. In all probability these will catch again at first light.

In any case you must look at your snares as soon after first light as possible, not only in an attempt to thwart Reynard, but also for humanitarian reasons. Never, under any circumstances, set snares which you cannot inspect inside twenty-four hours.

As with netted rabbits, snared ones also will fetch a better price at the poulterer's.

Locating Your Snares

The more snares you have set, the more rabbits you are likely to catch. However, you must be certain that you know where they all are. When snaring hedges or fences you can always tie a small piece of string on branch or rail above each wire.

You will soon learn which are your best killing runs, but if you persist in having snares permanently set in the same place the rabbits will soon become wise to them. It is often a good policy to leave a good run unsnared for a few days every so often. This will pay handsome dividends when you start using it again.

Long-netting

Long-netting for rabbits is usually looked upon as a method employed by poachers, but this is not the case. It is a highly efficient way of controlling rabbits on your shoot, though not the most sporting. A hundred yards of this type of netting can be purchased for about £25. On an open field it is most effectively used on a moonless night. The net is stretched across an open field where rabbits are known to feed whilst a *well-trained* dog is used to drive the rabbits into the net.

This is a job for three persons, one to work with the dog whilst the other two will be kept fully employed *behind* the net, rushing to despatch rabbits every time they hear them in the net.

The long-net can also be used in conjunction with ferrets, particularly in hedgerows where the rabbits are disinclined to bolt into the open. Smaller lengths of this netting are stretched through the hedge, ten or fifteen yards on each side of the burrow. Even if it is not successful in catching those rabbits which may spot it, at least it will make them bolt into the open so that the guns can get a shot.

TRAPPING

The cruel gin-trap is now illegal and has been replaced by a humane type of rabbit-trap, the Fenn Mk. 1, which is officially approved *for setting in holes for rabbits.*

Details of this trap have been kindly supplied to the author by the makers, Messrs. A. Fenn, High Street, Astwood Bank, Redditch, Worcs., from whom these traps are obtainable direct.

GASSING

As mentioned earlier in this book, gassing is an operation carried out simply to reduce the numbers of rabbits in a particular area. Whilst we must recognise it as a necessity in some cases, we also deplore the wastefulness involved. Good meat rots underground and the sportsman is deprived of a worthwhile quarry.

Nevertheless, with complaints pouring in from surrounding farmers, and the majority of his rabbit warrens in cover that defies ferreting or shooting, the amateur gamekeeper may well find himself having to undertake this task. However, the Ministry of Agriculture or your local branch of the National Farmers' Union should be consulted first.

Cymag is a form of powder which gives off a lethal gas when it becomes moist. *It is highly dangerous and the utmost care is needed.*

Your equipment is simple, a tin of gas, a spade and a long-handled spoon with which to place the powder in the burrows.

Keep the tin tightly closed at all times and only operate in dry weather. A whiff of this gas will cause you to vomit and any quantity inhaled could be fatal!

Having located the burrow, block up all the holes except the one in which you will introduce the gas. The lid of the tin is quickly opened, a spoonful of powder taken out, and closed up again. Deposit the Cymag as far as possible down the rabbit hole, and then block the entrance up quickly. The dampness of the earth is sufficient to cause the gas to evaporate from the powder in a very short time.

Do not attempt to open up that burrow for at least a week. Most operators leave it to the next colony of rabbits, but if you do reopen the holes you will probably find several dead rabbits close to the surface where they have been attempting to scratch their way to freedom before the fumes finally overcame them.

Personally, I detest gassing rabbits, and much prefer the following method on terrain where the burrows are to be found in dense cover.

MOBILE RABBITING

"Rabbit-control" sets most shooting men and landowners a problem. Where in pre-war times a farmer accepted the fact that he had a colony of rabbits on his land, today he is not prepared to do so, indeed he is not *allowed* to do so. Once it is brought to the notice of the authorities that rabbits are in abundance in a certain area, the owner or occupier of that land has to destroy them in the most effective, legal manner in which he is able. This may sound simple to the man behind the desk who has ordered the destruction of a certain rabbit population, but to the man on the spot, whose job it is to execute these orders, it is an entirely different story.

Ideal weather and vehicle for "mobile rabbiting"

The author rents five hundred acres of woodlands, consisting mainly of thick conifer plantations and, once the rabbits are on the increase there, problems arise in no small way. Ferreting has been attempted on numerous occasions, with very little success. First, one may have to crawl on hands and knees—for anything up to three hundred yards—into the various plantations, before the warrens are located. There is not enough room to shoot under the trees, so one has to rely on purse-nets. This may sound simple enough, but one is not able to move speedily enough under these conditions to reach a rabbit in a net before it has a chance to free itself, and in nine cases out of ten, in such an area, one overlooks at least one bolt hole, and has the frustration of seeing one's quarry vanishing into the wood.

Snaring, too, has been attempted with only a small amount of success, the snag here being that in an area like this there are thousands of "runs" to choose from, and short of setting a limitless number of wires to be visited daily, it cannot be conducted effectively. Gassing, in an impenetrable area, is probably better than both ferreting and snaring, but the author always regards it as rather a defeatist's attitude towards a rabbit population, when there is an ample supply of edible, saleable rabbit meat available.

The writer has reduced a large rabbit population by means of shooting them, during the hours of darkness, from a vehicle. The sportsman will frown, and click his tongue, but let him remember that, first and foremost, this is not a sporting operation. It is purely and simply rabbit control, aimed solely at reducing the numbers where other methods have failed, in an effort to protect crops and forestry.

GAME MUST NOT BE DISTURBED

However, this method of shooting the coney in the headlights of a vehicle is not the slaughter which it may, at first, appear to be. It took several weeks to adjust to this form of shooting, and it was simply a case of trial and error.

In terrain such as this, any pheasants which happen to be roosting in the woods will be deep in the fir thickets, and will not be disturbed by gunfire at night. There are no partridges, so there is no fear of sending them whirring into a barbed-wire fence as could easily happen on open fields. All one is likely to encounter are rabbits and hares, and compared with the useful job being carried out, the exercise can do very little harm to the resident game. One must bear in mind that hares are game, and therefore it is illegal to shoot them between the hours of sunset and sunrise. It is always a good idea, before attempting a foray of this nature, to have a word with the local police in case there should be any bye-laws preventing this type of shooting.

Difficulty in Judging Range

On the first attempt to shoot rabbits with the aid of headlights, it was discovered that the guns were killing about one to every four shots, and it was difficult to understand how simple shots such as these were being missed. It was on the second shoot that everyone realised where they were going wrong. The headlights were extremely powerful when on "full beam", and one is apt to take for granted that rabbits held in the lights are automatically in range. The guns had been shooting at some, possibly eighty yards away, fully believing them to be no farther than fifty.

Teamwork

Night shooting from a vehicle is based mainly on teamwork. The driver is the key man on whom success depends, for it is he who will search out the rabbits and manoeuvre the vehicle into the easiest position for a shot. Always remember that unless the ground is exceptionally level, it is imperative to pull up for each shot. Most Land Rovers have a very convenient tail-board which makes an ideal platform for the shooter. He must be as comfortable as possible, and have ample vision if all the chances offered are to be capitalised upon. Therefore, whilst the driver and shooter constitute the main body of the team, a third member can add to its efficiency. The bags in question were increased by having someone in the front passenger seat with a movable spotlight, wired to the battery, to pick out those rabbits which either ran out of the headlight beams, or sat still on high banks where they would otherwise remain unseen.

Three persons are the maximum number for a rabbiting team such as this. Do not encourage passengers or spectators, for this increases the risk of accidents, a very real danger at any time when vehicles and guns are used in conjunction.

Picking Up

It is always preferable for the shooter himself to pick up the rabbits he has shot. He knows exactly where they are and, should one recover and attempt to run off, he is on hand to give it a second barrel. The author remembers one occasion, some years ago, when he went out with four farmers in a pick-up truck after rabbits on some grazing land. It was a nightmare ride, and in one corner of a field they sighted four rabbits. Three rolled over to six barrels, and the writer jumped down to pick-up. As he approached the rabbits, one began hopping away. As he made to run after it there was a thunderous report from the truck, a charge of shot whistled past his head, and the rabbit rolled over, about three yards away from him. Consequently, he is reluctant to join in these type of shoots with strangers, and prefers his own "hand-picked" team.

Snow is Ideal

Conditions are as important in this type of shooting as in any other. A wet night is useless and is merely a waste of petrol. A dry, frosty night is ideal, and a light covering of snow is excellent. The best ever bag was made on this particular acreage when six inches of snow lay on the ground, but one must have a vehicle fitted with "four-wheel-drive" to undertake this with any degree of safety. Snow is helpful in so much as the target shows up plainly, even when out of the beam of the headlights, and it is sometimes possible to dispense with the movable spotlight.

This type of shooting, although not sporting in the strict sense of the word, can be a very enjoyable way of carrying out an extremely necessary job. Providing the game does not suffer on account of it, and the legal aspects have been investigated beforehand, there is no harm in it whatsoever.

RATTING

There must be no sentiments where ratting is concerned. Whilst the ferreter develops a respect and admiration for the rabbit, he will find only loathing in his heart for the rat. Yet the latter is certainly a more cunning quarry.

The terrier is an ideal ally on a ratting expedition

Do Not Use Young Ferrets for Ratting

Young ferrets must never be used for ratting. The two species are natural enemies, and the rat will seize its opportunity to kill an inferior enemy.

Where ferrets are to be used for ratting, it is a good idea to feed them a dead rat from time to time, reminding them of their most hated enemy.

No Muzzles or Lines for Ratting

Lined or muzzled ferrets are at a great disadvantage where rats are the quarry. Rats are not bolted easily like rabbits, often preferring to stand their ground and fight.

Use a Force of Ferrets

You will need more than one or two ferrets. It will be a fierce battle with many fights, and from time to time tired and injured ferrets will have to be replaced.

Weapons

Most ratting expeditions will be carried out in the proximity of a farm—either in the barns or in the rickyard. Indoors, of course, it is dangerous to use a firearm, and the bolted rats will have to be dealt with by terriers or sticks and shovels.

Out-of-doors, though, it will be more sporting. A .410 or a small No. 3 bore garden-gun are ideal. It is a good test for the young marksman, but safety must be strictly adhered to. There will be people, terriers and ferrets rushing to and fro, and only clear shots must be taken. Adult supervision is essential.

Start Early

The earlier you start, the better, for unlike rabbiting where a warren can be worked in a matter of a comparatively short time, rats will be reluctant to leave their holes, and just when you think it is all over, more will start to bolt.

Block up as many holes as you can beforehand. There will be many unseen ones, and you must attempt to cover the main exits.

Treat Ferrets' Wounds Afterwards
There is an old superstition that a ferret bitten by a rat will die, but this is entirely untrue. You must, however, examine your ferrets afterwards and treat all wounds with TCP. This superstition probably originated because many ferrets died from untreated wounds in olden times.

RABBITING OR RATTING?

A constant subject for debate amongst ferreters is whether ferrets used for ratting are spoiled for rabbiting.

Unfortunately, there is no positive answer to this question. Some claim that those which have been used for ratting work rabbit warrens much more thoroughly, whilst others insist that their ferrets are more prone to lying-up, being that much more eager for the kill.

* * *

Ferreting is a sport which requires perseverance. One never stops learning. Each expedition brings something new to the notice of the ferreter. Lady Luck, too, plays her part. Sometimes the novice bags a large number of rabbits whilst his more experienced counterpart has a blank day under identical conditions.

It is factors such as these which appeal to our sporting instincts. Whatever the day yields, we are always determined to do better next time.

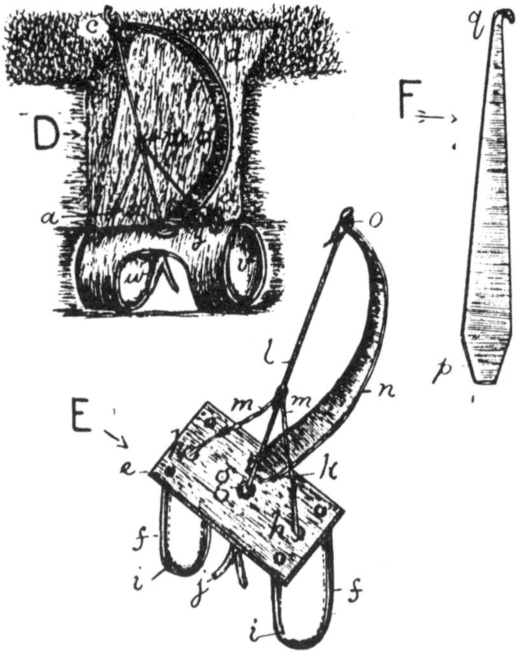

The Kent Garden Tube and Board-top Mole Traps

D, tube trap: v, tube; w, forked piece or table; x, table and spring string-hole; y, flat eye to receive lower end of spring; z, knot on main string where snare strings secured; 1, point where wire-snares affixed to snare-strings; b, steel spring; c, loop of main string affixed on hook of spring, thus the main main string held by table is tight and the snare strings slack so as not to disturb wire snares inside tube; d, slope made in soil so as to admit spring of trap; E, board-top trap; e, ½in. board, preferably hardwood; f, bows; g, main string and table hole; h, snare holes; i, wires placed inside bows; j, forked piece or table; k, flat eye for spring; l, main string (tight); m, snare strings (slack); n, steel spring; o, loop of main string passed over hook of spring; F, detached spring; p, wedge end; q, hook end.

Part Two:
TRAPPING

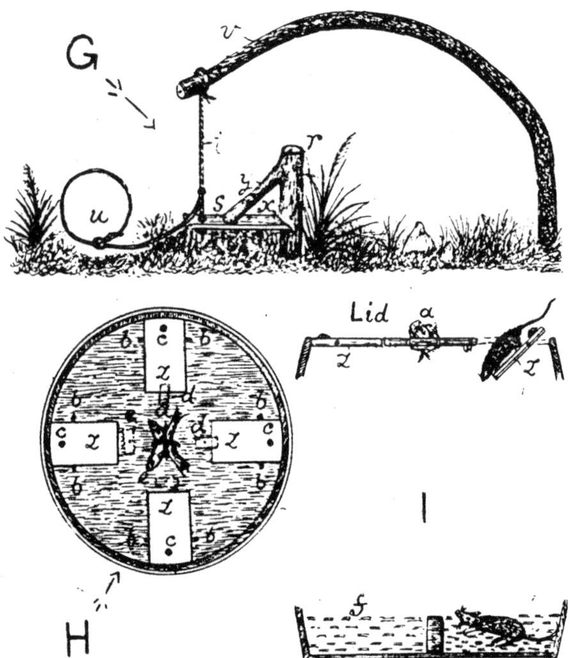

Snare-spring and Barrel Rat Traps

G, snare-spring trap; r, peg; s, straight stick; t, whipcord; u, wire noose; v, rod; w, rat run; x, notch; y, hook; H, barrel trap; z, falls; a, bait; b, pivots; c, lead; d, button turned under fall; e, the same turned from under fall; I, section of top and bottom of barrel; f. water

CHAPTER 6

The Trapper's Quarry

As already mentioned in this book, the only efficient means of controlling ground vermin on one's shoot is by *systematic* tunnel-trapping. We shall deal with the traps which may legally be used as well as mentioning those which are banned by law.

First, though, it is necessary that we know exactly which species are detrimental to game, and those which we are allowed to take by law, and the manner in which they can be trapped.

We have dealt with members of the weasel tribe in the first part of this book, so now we must consider other four-footed foes, as well as one or two feathered ones which can be taken in net or cage-traps.

GREY SQUIRREL

The grey squirrel is not a native of this country, but a creature from across the Atlantic. Originally, it escaped from captivity, bred prolifically and over the years was instrumental in reducing our own red squirrel almost to the point of extinction.

The grey squirrel is often described as a "tree-rat". This description is very apt. Its main diet is harmless enough—nuts, beech-mast and insects—yet it seems to have an insatiable appetite for game-birds' eggs and chicks, as well as doing immense damage to growing trees. It shows a preference for hardwood

Grey squirrel

forests, and wherever possible the dreys must be poked out with long poles, and the occupants shot as they climb towards safety.

Yet, the only sure way to reduce their numbers is with the tunnel-trap. Possibly the grey squirrel is the easiest of all vermin to trap on account of its curiosity and apparent lack of cunning. Grey squirrels frequent suburban gardens, and only recently the author was called upon to destroy some in such surroundings. Using a shotgun he accounted for four with the same number of shots, the creatures making no effort to flee the garden as he proceeded to shoot them.

THE HEDGEHOG

The hedgehog's chief enemies (apart from the motorist!) are the fox and the badger. The hedgehog (hedge-pig or Urchin, according to where you live) is a nomad who does not mind moving from one leafy corner to another. He does not necessarily live in a hedgerow.

A Villain

However, Mr. Prickles has two sides to his character. Too often we imagine him as a great benefactor to the countryside, eating slugs, snakes and mice, and we are led to believe that this is his sole diet. Far from it.

Any gamekeeper will tell of the damage this seemingly innocent, slow-moving creature is capable of. His *favourite* diet is, without any doubt, *eggs!* He will by-pass all the slugs in the neighbourhood if he knows where there is a clutch of partridge or pheasant eggs. Furthermore, the hen bird has far less chance of defending her nest against his depredations than she has of fighting off the

The Hedgehog—A Jekyll and Hyde character

egg-thieves of the corvine tribe. The hedgehog will simply roll himself up into an impregnable ball and bulldoze her off the nest. He is equally as fond of poultry eggs, and often will manage to squeeze into a hen-house where he will help himself liberally. On many occasions, though, after a sumptuous feast, he has found it impossible to leave through the hole where he has gained entry and, consequently, is caught red-handed by the irate poultry-farmer next morning.

Thus, the hedgehog is a true Jekyll and Hyde, a villain at nesting-time in fields and coverts, yet almost always beneficial to the gardener. Often this creature is quite content to remain within the confines of a garden, especially if he is looked after and tempted to stay. The author remembers, one year, when he had a resident hedgehog in his spacious garden. Each evening he placed a saucer of bread and milk on the lawn, and then, after dark, checked by torchlight to ensure that Horace was still around. Then, one night, Horace brought his wife and four baby hedgepigs to feast with him. Where their nest had been was never discovered.

Road Deaths

The roads claim the greatest toll of hedgehog deaths. During the summer it is almost impossible to drive more than a few miles without coming across at least one squashed carcase. Yet, this animal is not as slow-moving as one would imagine. He can cover short distances at amazing speeds, but a bright light at night causes him to halt in his tracks and roll himself up into a ball. Of course, his prickles are no defence against the wheels of cars, and how many stretches of roads are without vehicles for any length of time, even in the dead of night?

The hedgehog's prickles are not his only means of defence. When danger threatens he will emit an obnoxious smell in the same way as the skunk and the polecat. However, this is designed to repel furred and feathered foes, and it may not always be noticeable to the human intruder. One can, however, sometimes hear him snoring on a calm, windless day, in a quiet rural area.

Hedgehog on the Menu!—Many years ago, in the era of roaming bands of gipsies (Romanies, not motorised tinkers!) the hedgehog was a favourite dish. Their method of preparation was to roll the dead creature up in clay, then bake it in a slow fire. The clay would harden and, when split, both prickles and skin would come away with it. An old countryman who had once feasted thus at a gipsy campfire, said that the hedgehog, cooked in this method, is most palatable, and is not unlike pork. Whilst mentioning the prickles, it must be emphasised that they are merely hairs, $\frac{3}{4}$ in. in length, which harden as the hedgehog gains maturity.

On the increase.—The hedgehog is possibly one of the few creatures in this modern age which is rapidly increasing in certain parts of the country. Perhaps, without the motorist, we might even have a surplus, or a plague of them, depending upon whether one is a gardener, gamekeeper or poultry-farmer.

MOLE

It is surprising how little is known about the mole. He is not an easy animal to study, and naturalists are hampered by the fact that this creature spends virtually the whole of its life below ground. Many people have never even seen one of these interesting

The Mole—A destructive tunneller

little creatures, although most are able to identify its presence in a garden for the mole is one of the biggest nuisances to gardeners and farmers as it tunnels below the surface, pushing up unsightly piles of earth at intervals as it goes. A farmer can shut up his poultry securely to keep a fox or stoat out, but there is no way of locking a mole out of a field or garden.

A fully grown adult mole is capable of tunnelling up to 100 yards per day, the forelegs being shaped like natural spades, thereby making this possible. He will consume between fifty and sixty earthworms daily, often the equivalent of his own weight, but he enjoys a varied diet, and will also devour such delicacies as dead birds, mice, voles, etc., which he may find on his occasional expeditions above ground.

The mole is *not* completely blind as some people are inclined to believe, but is only able to tell the difference between light and darkness. However, he is compensated for this poor eyesight by most acute senses of hearing and smell. Above ground he gives the appearance of "swimming" over the surface, and is a very swift traveller in this manner. He can also swim in water, and is not unduly concerned about spells of hard weather, simply burrowing deeper below the surface.

Moles are ferocious creatures, and if two moles happen to meet they will often fight to the death. This is hardly surprising for their tunnels allow little scope for retreat.

The Mole-catcher

Rarely, today, does one come across the old-fashioned mole-catcher, probably the one man who knew and understood these creatures far better than all the scientists and naturalists. He worked with traps, and knew where to find the most-used runs out of a field covered with mole-hills. The only evidence which the layman saw of his work would be the rows of corpses hung from the surrounding fences as proof of this man's efficiency. Nowadays, it is mostly Ministry operators who look after the job of keeping the mole population in check, the main weapon of war being the earthworm dosed with strychnine. Each spring and autumn, in certain areas, one can see fields covered with mole heaps, these being particularly noticeable on pastureland. Yet, it is amazing just how few moles are responsible for this unsightliness. One mole can cause a tremendous amount of damage in this way, particularly amongst growing crops or on lush turf, and only the experienced mole-catcher will know where to place his traps most effectively. An amateur is liable to waste an awful lot of time for poor results.

Shooting Moles

I heard of a farmer who had been reducing the number of moles on his land by means of shooting them with a twelve-bore. He spent many hours waiting and watching in his orchard where the moles were particularly industrious. As soon as he saw any movement amongst a heap of soil he blasted into it from a range of about a yard. This method was reasonably successful, and one day he succeeded in killing four moles.

An Old Belief.—There is an old belief that if a mole receives a cut on his sharp pointed snout he will die. Some old countrymen used to place lengths of bramble in the tunnels, but there is no proof of the success of this method because a mole which spends most of its life tunnelling through soil is sure to receive the odd cut from time to time, and therefore must be reasonably immune to it.

Sometimes Cats Will Kill Moles.—The writer had some trouble with a particular mole in his own garden many years ago. Having attempted unsuccessfully to trap it, he was surprised one morning to find it lying dead on the lawn without a mark on it. How had it died? If it was from natural causes then surely death would have occurred below ground. One can only surmise on how it met its untimely end, but possibly it had surfaced in search of a change of diet, and had met a swift death at the claws of a prowling cat. One swipe of a paw would have been sufficient to kill this small mammal without a trace, and then the cat, not fancying this meal, had left its kill lying there.

Moles in Captivity.—It is tempting for a young person who manages to catch a live mole to keep it as a pet. This has been tried unsuccessfully many times by children, but the main problem is providing it with sufficient food. It is a fortunate person who is able to supply a mole with somewhere in the region of four hundred earthworms per week!

It is a great pity that an interesting little fellow like the mole enjoys such a degree of unpopularity and is constantly hounded by Man. Were it not for his untidy excavations he would, no doubt, be left in peace.

WINGED VERMIN WHICH MAY LEGALLY BE TRAPPED

There are methods by which winged vermin can be legally trapped, and in the following chapter this subject will be covered. Also, the illegal pole-trap will be described, surely the most cruel of all traps, outlawed since the early part of this century.

However, it is necessary for the beginner to have some knowledge of the habits of winged vermin, the numbers of which he must attempt to control either by cage-trap, net-trap or gun.

Carrion Crow

The carrion crow demands a solitary existence, choosing the highest branches of some solitary tree in which to rear its evil brood, instructing them from the moment they first learn to use their wings that the eggs and young of smaller birds are a delicacy much preferable to carrion and garbage gleaned from refuse tips.

The carrion crow is easily distinguished from the rook by its larger size, jet black colour from beak to tail-feathers, and the fact that it is always to be seen hunting alone. Its croak, too, is that much deeper.

Whilst the rook atones for much of its natural predatory instincts by its usefulness towards agriculture in that its diet consists of harmful forms of life, such as wire-worms, gleaned by following the plough, the carrion crow has no such traits to cause the game-preserver to view it with a friendly eye at any time of the year. In common with the rest of the corvine tribe it is a slow flier with sharp eyesight, and a clutch of eggs has to be exceptionally well concealed in order to escape its attentions. Furthermore, if its own nest is discovered and destroyed by a gamekeeper it is sufficiently persistent in its efforts to rear its young that it will build elsewhere and hatch a late brood. Such is the alertness of the female bird that it will glide to safety at the approach of danger, and only return when it is safe to do so. The eggs seem little effected by a prolonged absence, as is

Carrion Crow—An evil predator

borne out by a friend of mine who kept a carrion crow away from her nest for a full twenty-four hours, and then discovered that there were fledglings in the nest a week later!

Rook

By comparison, the rook is a much friendlier bird, and although it will ravage a nest of eggs if discovered during the course of its search for food, it appears to be quite content with a diet of grain, and that which the plough brings to the surface. However, it is necessary that some form of control is maintained annually, and nowadays this is left mostly to gamekeepers and sportsmen. Mention must be made of the traditional rook-shoots which took place on most estates up until a quarter of a century ago. Strangely, they seem to have died out, and one wonders if the humble rook has lost its place amongst the lesser sporting birds. May 12th was generally accepted as the opening date for rook-shooting, for by this time the majority of the young birds are capable of perching on the branches in the vicinity of their nests. The rookery was ringed by those who preferred to use shotguns, whilst the "marksmen", armed with specially manufactured "rook-rifles" or even .22s, moved amongst the trees, accounting for the "branchers", as the young rooks were termed. Meanwhile those rooks that had attained full powers of flight, and sought to escape, were accounted for by the shotgunners who also attempted to deal with the irate adult birds. No small amount of skill is required to bring down a young rook swaying precariously in the topmost branches of a tall tree, using a rifle, and a useful job of control was accomplished in the most sporting manner possible. Alas, today, control is left to the enthusiastic shooting man, and that once

The Rook

popular sporting and social function has become a thing of the past, when upwards of five hundred rooks would be shot on a warm May evening, and the delicacies of rook-pie were sampled over the ensuing days.

Need for Control.—In many areas the rook population has increased to alarming proportions and extensive control is necessary if the balance of Nature is to be maintained. It is in the interests of all game preservers to carry this out if the rook is still to be regarded as "the farmer's friend".

Magpie

Where a fine plumage is concerned, the magpie is second only to the jay amongst the corvine tribe, but when it comes to villainy he can often teach the wily carrion crow a trick or two. We have all seen the magpie at some time or other, particularly on a train or bus journey where his black and white markings show up plainly on the fields. During the winter months this bird is generally found in small flocks of up to a dozen, gleaning left-over grain from the barren fields. As far as the countryside is concerned, the magpie is then relatively harmless, but once spring arrives he becomes the villain which has earned him a place high on the "wanted" list of gamekeepers and conservationists.

The magpie's eyesight is amongst the keenest of all the birds and beasts of the countryside. The songsters which have taken an immense amount of trouble to camouflage their nests in the thickest of hedgerows and coppices, believing their eggs to be safe from predators, have reckoned without this their deadliest foe of all. The magpie is a patient egg-hunter, remaining concealed in the thickets for hours until a

The Magpie—A noisy villain

slight movement catches his sharp eye. A sitting thrush or blackbird—the plunder is a foregone conclusion.

Partridges and pheasants, too, suffer from the depredations of this black and white predator. Chicks which have survived the hatching stage are more vulnerable than ever now, for they are inclined to wander away from the protection of the hen, and they have no chance, whatsoever, when the magpie swoops down on them.

The magpie is ubiquitous, ranging throughout the British Isles, although sometimes he is more prevalent in one county than another. Common lands are an ideal place to go if you wish to see this bird in its natural surroundings, for the magpie is well aware that the gamekeeper cannot pursue him there. However, your only real chance of studying the magpie will be from a distance, through a pair of powerful binoculars, for he is wary of *all* humans. In woodlands he will see you before you see him, and you cannot mistake his chattering as he mocks you from the thickest covert. In this respect he is very similar to the jay, but in spite of their resemblance the two species do not mix. They may occupy the same wood, but their territories will be separate. Indeed, they seem to show a marked respect for each other.

A Thief.—The magpie is a thief as well as a predator. Once the nesting season is over he will extend his hunting area to the poultry farms in search of newly-laid eggs. If the farmer has forgotten to shut his hen-house door at night, the magpie will be on the scene at first light, and will enter the building. Often, on such a raid, he will fly off with an egg, and devour the yoke leisurely in some place of safety, rather than remain and suck the whole clutch as he would do in the case of a nest in the wild.

Anything which glitters attracts the magpie, and there have been instances where jewellery has been stolen from houses, and later discovered in a magpie's nest. The bird had obviously entered through an open window, and people who encourage this species to use their bird-tables are inviting a thief on to their premises.

Years ago, when a gamekeeper's gibbet was a regular feature of our countryside, magpies were always to be found hanging from it. Often the nature-lover became upset at the destruction of such a handsome bird, but had that person taken the trouble to study the habits of the magpie, his sympathy would have lessened. A magpie can destroy a whole clutch of songsters or gamebirds at one raid, and if constant war was not waged upon these predators by gamekeepers and conservationists, then the corvine tribe would rule the countryside. In time the smaller birds would be in danger of extinction, and instead of being awakened by a dawn chorus of songsters we should hear only the harsh chattering of magpies, the screeching of jays and the incessant "cawing" of their less colourful relatives.

At the same time, though, one must bear in mind that the balance of Nature has to be preserved, and the magpie plays an equal part in the country scene. Villain as he is, extermination is not the answer. We must aim simply at control.

JAY

The jay is high on the gamekeeper's vermin list. His favourite diet is eggs and newly hatched chicks. Skilful as the partridge and pheasant are at camouflaging their nests, they are fortunate if they can escape the sharp eye and evil attentions of this heartless robber.

The jay incurs a tremendous amount of sympathy from the casual visitor to the countryside. As they catch a brief glimpse of him flitting across a woodland ride with the shafts of sunlight scintillating on his bright plumage, they liken him to the parakeet. Surely such a beautiful bird is a valuable asset to our fields and coverts, they think, as they return to their urban dwellings.

However, it is mainly due to the efforts of the gamekeeper that the jays' numbers are controlled. Were it not for this guardian of field and covert, this bird's depredations would spread to suburban areas, where it would comb the hedgerows of gardens in search of tasty songbirds' eggs and chicks. Not realising the danger which it portended, the town-dweller would welcome such an attractive visitor to his bird-table.

However, it is not only wildlife which would suffer should the jay be allowed to breed prolifically. This corvine is very partial to peas with which to supplement its diet. The author once saw a field of peas which had attracted the attention of some jays. Marauding woodpigeons could hardly have equalled the damage. It is probable that the jay obtains as much pleasure from splitting the pods open as it does from eating the contents. In this case it was sheer corvine vandalism! There was row after row of split pods, and the peas which they had contained were simply strewn all over the ground.

Not to be Confused with the Magpie.—The jay is not to be confused with its nearest relative, the magpie. This latter has virtually the same traits, but is easily distinguished by its black and white plumage and

The Jay—An attractive plunderer

long tail. Whilst the jay shrieks harshly, the magpie chatters incessantly in a "machine-gun"-like fashion.

Yet, the task of the gamekeeper in controlling the jay population is far from easy. This cunning bird is a master of concealment, taunting man from amidst the thickets, flitting from branch to branch, and rarely presenting itself as a target for the keeper's gun.

The gamekeeper must match cunning with cunning. He must be abroad before daylight, hidden in that part of the wood where he knows that jays abound. If he is lucky he may get *one* shot, and he must make it count. Once the other jays know that Man, their most feared enemy, is within their domain, they will flit silently to the safety of another wood, returning only when he has gone.

Our most effective weapon is, undoubtedly, the net or cage trap.

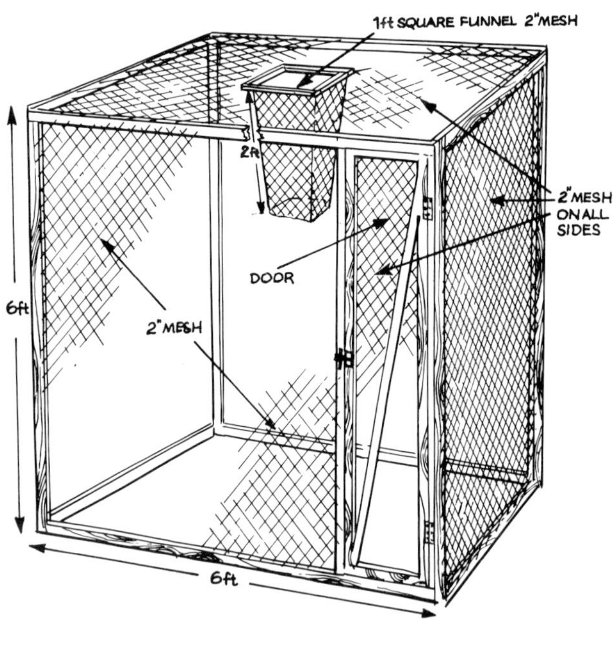

An easy-to-make crow and rook trap

CHAPTER 7

Traps and Trapping

ILLEGAL TRAPS

Just as the man-trap, the most devilish instrument ever invented or used, has found its way into the museums, so have the gin-trap and the pole-trap which followed in its wake.

The Pole-trap

The pole-trap is, in effect, nothing more than a circular gin-trap so designed that it can be placed on a

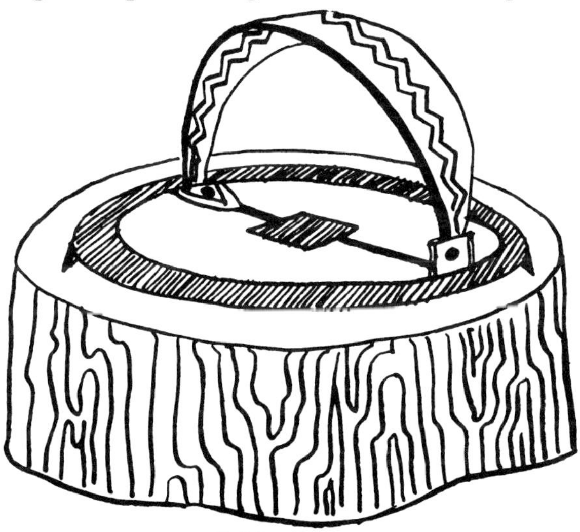

POLE-TRAP
another variation of the Gin, set on a pole or level tree stump.

tall pole or in the fork of a tree. Mostly these were baited with meat or carrion, and their success in catching birds of prey and members of the corvine tribe was unequalled. Nevertheless, much suffering was involved, and often birds were caught by the legs and left hanging upside down until the trapper decided to go and inspect his traps. The type of man who used these "engines" in the first place was hardly one to worry over added cruelty.

The Gin-trap

There were two sizes of gin-trap on the market up to 25 years ago. The larger, heavier variety was designed for the catching of foxes or badgers, often placed in the open with maybe three or four set around the remains of a dead lamb. Invariably, the gin always caught its larger victims by the leg, and many a fox has escaped at the expense of a severed limb, only to die a horrible lingering death later.

The smaller type was for use against rabbits and small ground vermin. The warreners, who have already been mentioned, used these extensively, setting them in rabbit holes and covering the open teeth with sand. Apart from the humane aspect, the snare was more versatile in as much that a hundred could be carried easily on one's person whereas a couple of dozen gins presented a formidable load.

It must be added, in all fairness, that when used in tunnels for stoats and weasels, etc., often death was instantaneous. However, modern humane traps have done away with the majority of the cruelty involved in trapping, and we must learn to use the Fenn traps, Mk. 1 and Mk. 4 respectively, in an efficient and humane manner.

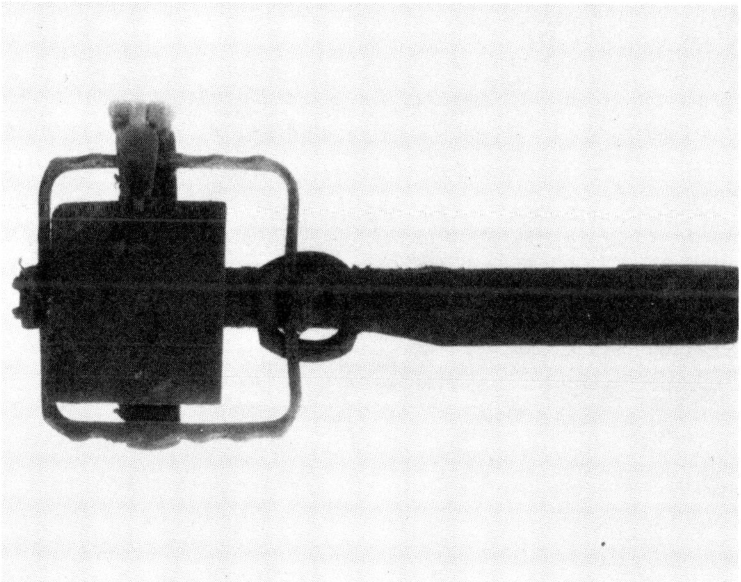

Gin-trap in *set* position—looking from above

Gin-trap in *sprung* position

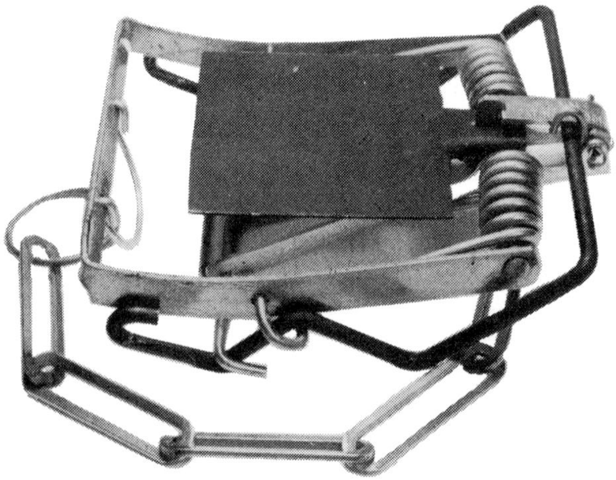

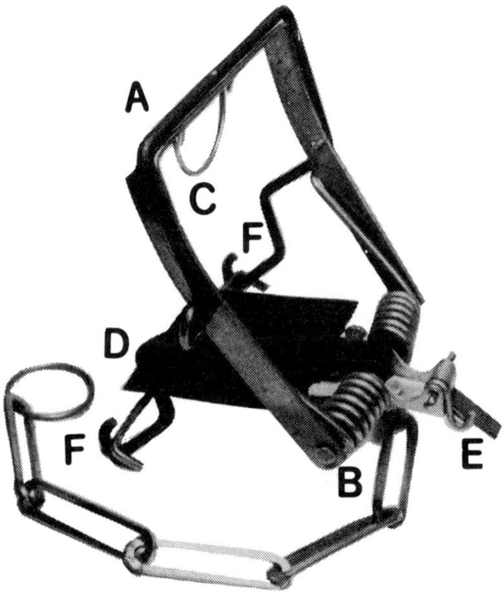
A
C
F
D
F
E
B

Humane Traps

We have already discussed the use of the Mk. 1 trap, and now we must look at the Mk. 4, obtainable direct from the makers, Messrs. A. Fenn, High Street, Astwood Bank, Redditch, Worcs.

It is light and easy to carry and, provided it is set correctly—in tunnels frequented by ground vermin—then good results should be obtained.

The reader must familiarise himself with the directions for setting before attempting to use these traps, and must also understand that *it is illegal to use them on birds.*

The author recalls an instance, over a decade ago, when he accidentally sprung one of these Mk. 4 traps, and trapped his thumb, entirely due to his own carelessness in not using the safety hook. Some pain and extensive bruising followed, but had he been using a gin-trap permanent injury would undoubtedly have been the result. This is yet another reason why we should rejoice at the demise of the gin.

Instruction in the Use of the Fenn Mk. 4 Humane Trap

To Set.—Place left thumb in loop C, with fingers under base D. Right thumb on bar A, with fingers under spring B. Squeeze with both hands to fully open jaws, swing safety hook E over bar A, which prevents jaws closing. Both hands are now free to adjust brass catches taking care not to disengage safety hook, which is for your protection. Please use it.

Place trap in run with brass catch to the side and treadle in centre at ground level. Disengage safety hook when setting is completed.

Traps should be sprung and re-set occasionally if

nothing is caught.

Vermin may be released from the trap if necessary by turning trap over, pressing with foot or hand at base D and disconnecting hooks F.

RABBIT TRAP

A variety of rabbit traps, apart from the gin, were available to the warrener before the last war. The one illustrated here is typical of these, and has no safety device. It is heavy and cumbersome.

Instruction in the Use of the Fenn Mk. 1 Rabbit Trap

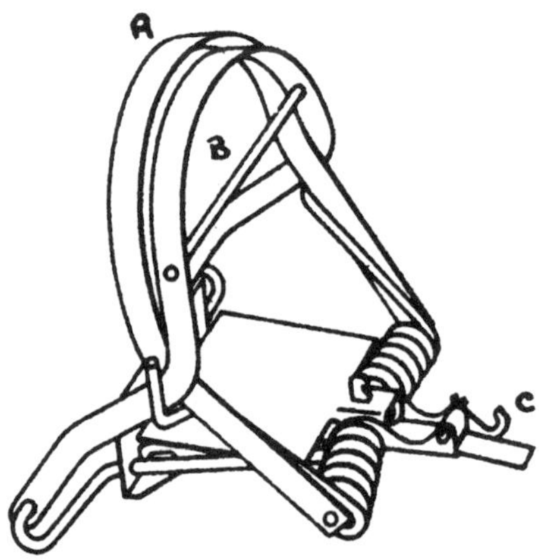

To Set.—Place trap on a firm surface, open safety hook C and brass flap. Place ball of thumb on top jaw A and press downwards, pulling crossbar B on other jaw with other hand at the same time. When jaws are open far enough flick safety hook over crossbar to prevent jaws closing. Press further and engage brass catches. These should be set fairly hard for catching full grown rabbits and lighter for young ones in summer.

Take care not to disengage safety hook until setting has been completed, then use a small stick in preference to your fingers.

The jaws extend 5 in. above the treadle (can be made 5½ in. if required for large holes or sandholes). Make sure traps have room to operate but the jaws should almost touch the top of the hole when sprung, this can be ensured by partly filling large holes with soil or placing the traps farther in. Failure to do this can result in rabbits going over the top without getting caught, or being foul caught.

It is a waste of time setting outside holes—apart from being illegal. Any difficulty in releasing a capture can be overcome by unhooking the springs from the jaws at the base of the trap.

Trapping is usually most effective in deep burrows, the best holes being trapped and the rest blocked. The method preferred for these traps is to fill in all burrows to be trapped a few days earlier, then trap those holes that have been re-opened. This saves a lot of time when setting and rabbits will be less suspicious of disturbance caused. If a large area is being trapped it is usual to move some of the traps to other burrows after two or three nights, and leave a few behind to pick up any rabbits that move back.

NET TRAP

The small spring-type net-trap is reasonably efficient against the corvine tribe which we have mentioned in the last chapter. The author has used one for many years and found it most effective during the nesting season when baited with crock eggs. A "nest" can be made up, incorporating the trap, with one egg fixed to the plate by means of a rubber band. On one occasion a carrion crow was found to be caught within ten minutes of setting.

Net-trap set for corvines, baited with crock egg. Iron pegs must be hammered well into the ground

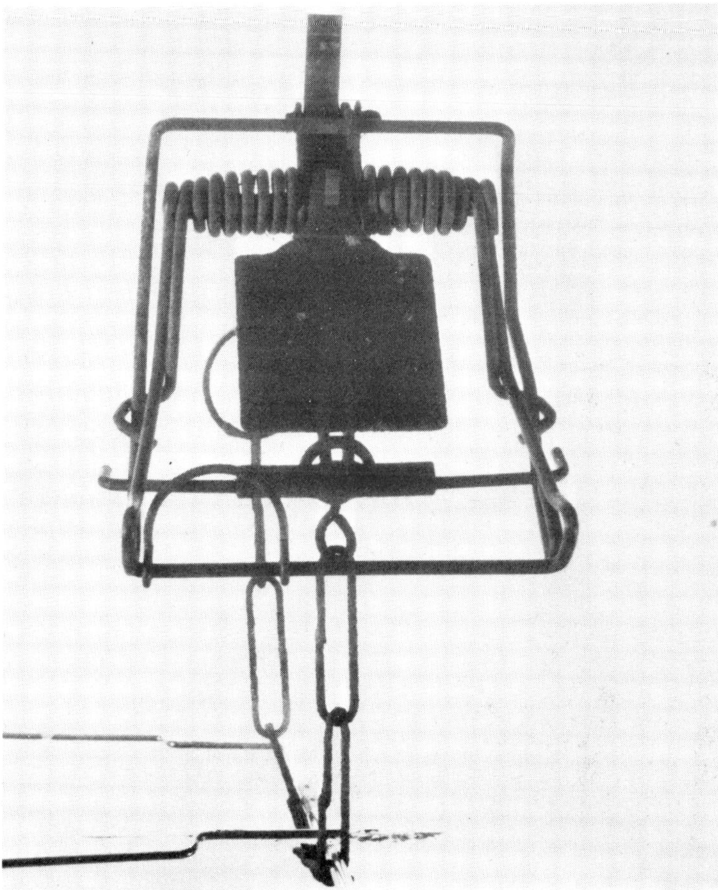

The Fenn Mk. 4 Humane Trap in "set" position with safety catch on

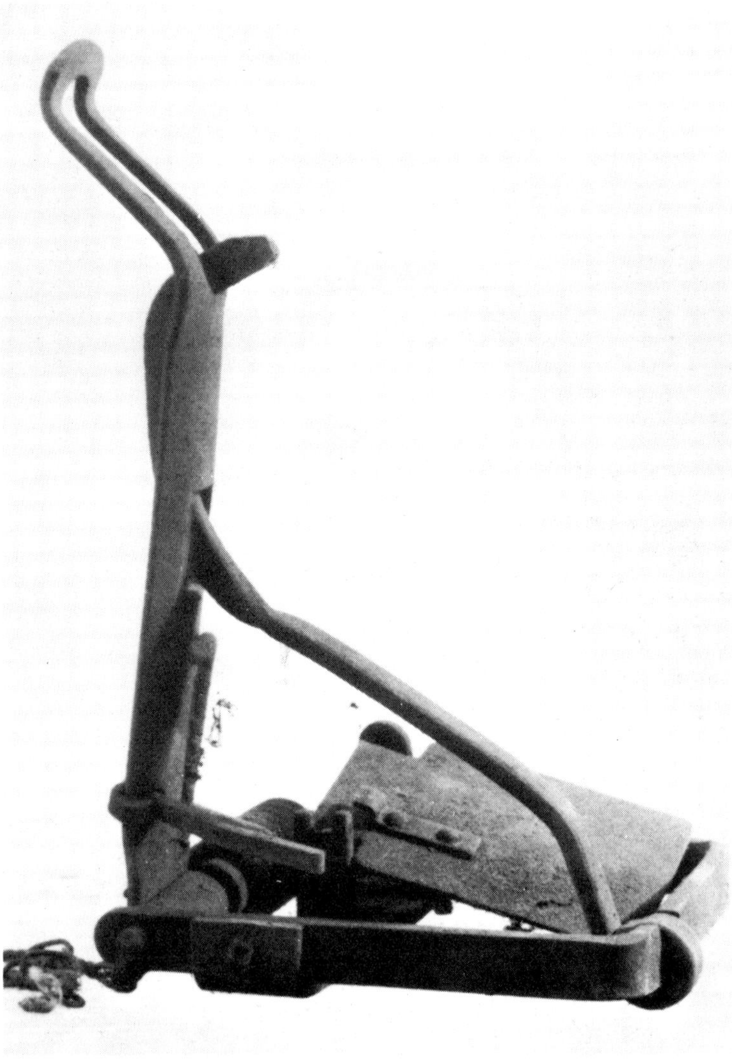

An old rabbit trap, the kind sometimes used by the warreners in preference to the gin-trap

Undergrowth surrounding a pool. Ideal place for either cage-type rat-trap or net-trap for corvines

Type of trap used by the old bird-catchers. Note call-bird in lower section

The only real drawback with this type of net device is that it regularly catches hedgehogs which become hopelessly entangled in the mesh during their struggles to free themselves. One can imagine the difficulties involved in attempting to extricate Mr. Prickles. The model illustrated was supplied by Gilbertson & Page Ltd. of Colney Heath. At present it is out of production, due to scarcity of parts.

THE CLAP-TRAP

Little is seen of the clap-trap today. It was once the main means (apart from bird-lime) by which the bird-catchers of old secured their songbirds for the market. Doubtlessly it could be effectively used against winged vermin, but the trapper would have to wait in a place of concealment in order to operate it. We can, therefore, discount this from our trapping equipment.

THE CAGE-TRAP

This device was dealt with at length in the author's book *Gamekeeping and Shooting for Amateurs.* Basically, this trap consists of a wire-netting enclosure, the measurements of which should be no less than 6 ft. by 6 ft. and the same height. A tapering funnel is constructed in the roof by which the crows enter, enticed by bait, but they are unable to leave by it as their open wings, necessary for take-off, are unable to pass through it. A door in the side of the cage enables the catches to be removed *daily.*

The only time during which this type of trap is really effective is during a spell of hard weather.

CAGE-TYPE RAT-TRAP

A very useful device which can be safely used anywhere on the shoot but, like the crow-trap, is most

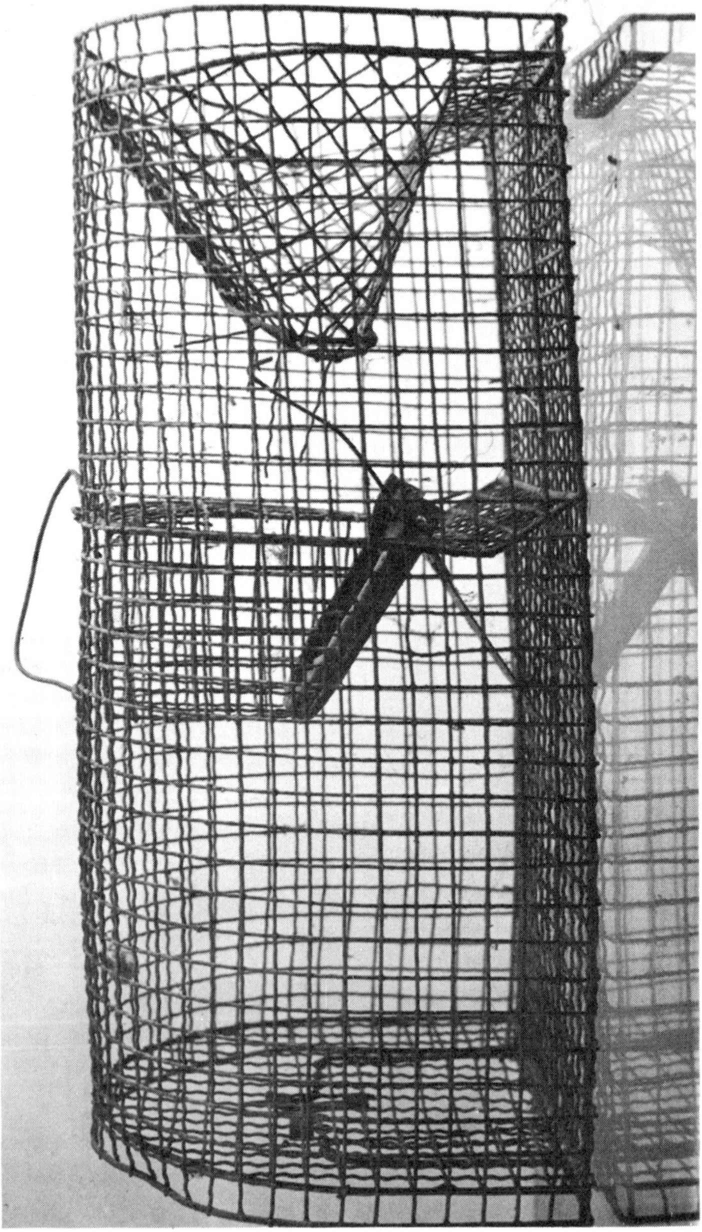

Cage-type rat-trap

Cage-type rat-trap showing entrance tunnel and drop-plate

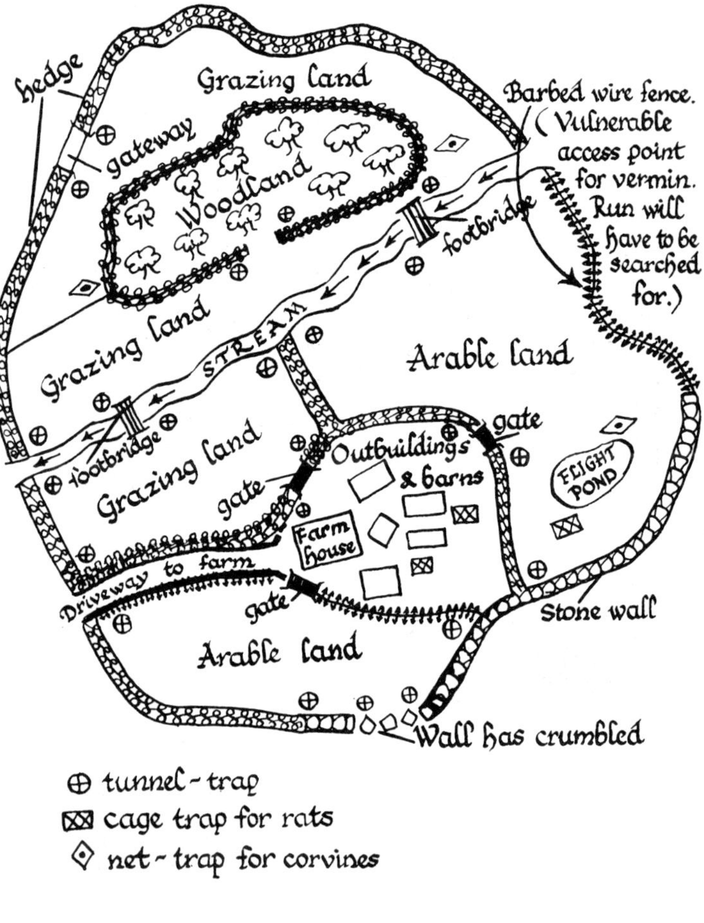

PLAN FOR TRAPPING
ON APPROXIMATELY 100 ACRES

Ground vermin will seldom cross open spaces unless it is inevitable. Take full advantage of a fence such as this, trapping on both sides of the wide ride

effective during cold weather. It has been known to catch the odd stoat or weasel, and the catches are most easily despatched by dropping the cage into a tank of water or a nearby pool or stream.

TUNNEL-TRAPPING

As stated before this is by far the most effective method of combating ground vermin. However, a plan of campaign must be carefully drawn up beforehand, and a sketch map of your shoot will be an invaluable aid.

PLACES TO SET TUNNEL-TRAPS

The most important factor to be borne in mind is that ground vermin seldom cross open spaces unless it is absolutely unavoidable. They will use every vestige of cover to reach their destination, and was it not for this, the work of the trapper would be exceedingly difficult.

Runs through hedgerows, gaps in stone walls, corners of buildings, and footbridges crossing a stream are all ideal places in which to trap stoats, weasels and grey squirrels. It will be seen from the diagram of a lay-out of an imaginary shoot that all these places have been covered, and that an attempt has been made to "defend" the entire boundary in an effort to trap vermin moving in from neighbouring land.

DO NOT UNDERESTIMATE THE WORK INVOLVED

Traps must be inspected daily, twice if possible, morning and evening, and you must not underestimate your duties. If you have a large acreage do not put out more traps than you can manage. There are times, particularly when traps are not catching well, that the job will become irksome, but you must not let-up if you are to stand any chance of producing a reasonable head of game.

WHEN TO TRAP

Hard weather is always best for tunnel-trapping, and this is the time to maintain a full complement of traps. During the summer months—when you will possibly be engaged in rearing duties—it will be as well just to keep traps in the best catching places. Certainly, though, you will need them in close proximity to your rearing-field. During the spring you can concentrate on attempting to reduce the numbers of your winged predators with a spring net-trap. It is hoped that before long these traps will be on the market again, but in the meantime it is possible to make an improvised one for yourself.

MAKING A NET-TRAP

One of these traps is quite simply constructed by using a gin-trap, with the teeth filed off, as a base. It is necessary, though, to use a "double" net, the two-halves meeting together when the plate is pressed. The job is completed in a matter of minutes with the aid of an electric drill. All that is needed then is to screw in two frames which meet when the trap is triggered off, covered with strong garden netting.

MAKING TUNNELS FOR TRAPS

Wooden tunnels in a complete unit halve the work of trapping. All that is necessary is for three pieces of wood of identical measurements, say 2 ft. long by 6 in. wide, to be nailed together to form two sides and a top. They can be painted a dark green, or perhaps even green and brown to blend in with the background, and this saves the time-consuming job of disturbing and rebuilding elaborate stone and earth tunnels. It is also a good idea to secure the chain of the trap to this tunnel. A stoat or weasel will not take it very far!

Pieces of large drain-piping will also serve adequately as tunnels.

Siting

It is not sufficient simply to place one of these tunnels anywhere on the shoot. Although our quarry are all curious by nature, they will only show interest in a "straight-through" tunnel if it is somewhere where they will encounter it upon their travels. Therefore, it is best sited along a stone wall, by a gatepost, or in close proximity to a footbridge. When pheasant poults are in a release-pen it is imperative to operate these tunnels on the *outside* of the wire. Vermin will hunt the perimeter in search of a means of entrance.

We must at all times take precautions to ensure that harmless forms of wildlife do not become caught in our traps. An inquisitive blackbird, thrush or pheasant poult is just as likely to get caught if we do not take steps to prevent this happening. Two or three sticks, stuck in the ground at the entrance to the tunnel, will allow small vermin access whilst keeping out birds and domestic animals.

BAITED TRAPS

Usually it is not necessary to bait vermin traps. Placed in the tunnel, and lightly covered with leaves (soil is inclined to impede the action and also promotes rust), curiosity itself should be the downfall of our intended victims.

However, there are occasions when our preserves are suffering from the depredations of a particularly

This gatepost is in an ideal place to catch ground vermin in tunnel-traps. They will follow the line of the fence before crossing the ride

cunning stoat or weasel, and it is necessary to remove the danger without delay.

Use a "blind" tunnel, i.e. block up one end of a tunnel with a clod of earth that cannot be easily moved. Beyond the trap in the blocked tunnel is your bait. A dead rabbit, or even its entrails, is ideal. Blood is always a good draw for the weasel-tribe—some sprinkled around the open entrance to the tunnel, and over the trap, should do the trick. Oil of musk, available from most chemists, is also a good lure for stoats and weasels.

LOOK FOR REGULAR RUNS

With some experience the game preserver should be able to recognise vermin runs quite easily. However, a fall of snow will facilitate this, and as soon as possible in such conditions one should be out and about on one's shoot, setting as many traps as possible, and also memorising those places which vermin frequent most. Soft fresh snow is also ideal for concealing a trap beneath. Fresh blood, too, will show up much more easily, and most butchers will readily supply you with a pint of this.

It is often an advantage to construct a "V" shaped "run-in" to tunnels by sticking rows of small branches in the earth on either side of the entrance. Vermin which would otherwise have passed your trap will be guided into the tunnel.

MAINTENANCE OF TRAPS

Spring Traps Regularly

Sometimes a trap will go for months without catching. Possibly it is badly sited, or else you have overdone a particular place and the vermin have become wise to it. In either case a fresh siting will be beneficial.

Sometimes, though, a trap must stay in place simply because its removal will break your "chain of defence". In this case it must be sprung regularly, at least once a week. If not, then it is likely to rust, and a light creature such as a weasel will be able to run over the plate without springing it.

Avoid Human Scent on Traps

Always keep a good reserve of traps and change them over at monthly intervals. Those brought in for "servicing" must be oiled and allowed to "weather" outside before being set in the tunnels again. Human scent is always liable to linger for a day or two and, in order to avoid delays in catching, gloves should be worn when handling traps.

Rats Along a Stream

If you have a stream on your land you will most certainly be troubled with rats. Whilst the Fenn Mk. 4 is ideal for killing these rodents, it may be preferable to use rat-cages where more than one creature can be taken at a time. It is best not to let the rats become accustomed to the sight of traps with rats caught in them, so place your traps just before dusk, and remove as soon as possible after first light. The occupants can be drowned in the stream providing it is deep enough.

Around the Feeding Points

However effective your boundary traps are, there will always be vermin around your feeding points, particularly grey squirrels. Great care must be taken here because pheasants will be in abundance (hopefully!) and your tunnels must be constructed in such a way that inquisitive poults cannot reach the traps.

Following a fall of snow is an ideal time to determine regular vermin runs

Grey squirrels are the easiest of all vermin to trap. Within a few hours of one being removed from a trap another will be caught. The author has caught them regularly with *uncovered* traps in tunnels, and it appears that so long as they can see daylight at the other end nothing stops them from entering.

MOLES

Moles are not strictly the quarry of the amateur gamekeeper, but it can only help to cement relationships with your landlord if you have a go at them from time to time.

Choose only the freshest mounds of earth amidst a maze of excavations and, instead of digging down with a spade, poke with a stout stick until you locate the hole. The less you disturb the original mole-hill the better, although you will have to widen the shaft with a small trowel to enable you to locate the crossing tunnel, the place where you must place your trap.

Once the trap is in position, fill the hole in until only the topmost part of the trap is visible. You will be able to tell by the position of this whether or not it has been sprung. As with all traps, you must inspect daily. However, it is seldom worthwhile resetting your trap in the same place. Look for another fresh mound. You will have more success there.

Dead Vermin

The successful trapper should be taking kills from his traps daily. Only he can decide on how these must be disposed of. Furriers will pay a few pence for stoat and weasel skins, as well as crow, rook, jay and magpie wings. It is possible to reclaim a small fraction of your outlay in this way. Otherwise you can bury the corpses, or else hang them up on a vermin gibbet in some discreet corner of the shoot where they will not be offensive to any member of the public chancing to

The mole trap

venture that way. A brief mention of gibbets will be worthwhile for the benefit of those readers who are not familiar with them.

Vermin Gibbets

In days gone by, when most of the large estates were privately owned, it was not unusual to see a gamekeeper's vermin "gibbet" situated, quite openly, on any acreage of land where organised shooting took place. To the uninitiated it was quite a gruesome sight, consisting of a length of rope stretched between two convenient trees, and on it would be hanging corpses of all species of wild life which the keeper considered were harmful to the game. Today many of these items of "vermin" have been placed on the "protected" list, and one no longer sees such birds as sparrow-hawks, kestrels and buzzards hanging in full view of public footpaths.

At one time an employer judged the merits of his gamekeeper by the number of head hanging in this unsightly line, and often the guardian of the fields and coverts was paid a bonus for his efforts. The keeper took a pride in this display, and often the bodies of stoats and weasels found their way on to an estate miles away from the one on which they had been killed! Possibly the squire would take a count of his servant's kills at the end of each month and, after the visit of inspection, the keeper would take most of the dead vermin to his counterpart on a neighbouring estate who was expecting his "check" during the coming week, and would earn himself an extra few shillings into the bargain. This was one way in which the system was abused, and many estate owners were cheated in this manner.

Birds classed as vermin, which rarely did much real harm, were wantonly killed by the keeper, merely for the bounty on their heads, and a species could, therefore, be in danger of becoming extinct. A buzzard, for instance, will take young pheasants when the opportunity presents itself, but its main diet is young rabbits. Nowadays it is afforded full protection by law. However, a "rogue" buzzard may develop a particular liking for young pheasant, and one could hardly blame a gamekeeper who took instant action once he realised where his young poults were disappearing to.

Vermin-gibbets are very much a relic of the past in this modern age, and many employers and shooting tenants will not tolerate them. However, there is no harm in a gamekeeper keeping one, provided it is in a *discreet* place where it may only be discovered by trespassers and others who have no right to be on the land in question. Provided that no bounty is paid, which might encourage the keeper to destroy wantonly, it is a good means of checking on whether he is in fact attending to his duty of vermin control. A lazy man may be inclined to neglect this task, and the only hint that this work was not being carried out would be the absence of game at the beginning of the following season. By then it would be too late, and the man concerned might be able to present all manner of plausible excuses to his boss for the scarcity of pheasants.

The maggots which fall from the rotting corpses of vermin which have paid the extreme penalty for their crimes are excellent food for pheasants, and this is probably the strongest case in favour of the gibbet.

Conclusion

Ferreting and trapping are but a small part of the very varied sport of shooting, yet they are vital cogs in a wheel that comprises a traditional rural pursuit.

Rabbit populations must be controlled if forestry and agriculture are to prosper, and vermin, likewise, must not be allowed to dominate the country scene otherwise gamebirds and songsters will become a diminishing species.

The amateur gamekeeper has an important role to play in helping to preserve the balance of Nature. Without him, those tracts of land unkeepered by the professional man would become a sanctuary for everything that is harmful to the way of life which we love most.

One never stops learning, and it is to be hoped that knowledge will be not wasted. The future of our sport is in our own hands, and we must maintain it for the next generation.

INDEX

Badger, 24
Badger Sett, 26, 27
Baited traps, 148, 150
Belgian Hares, 78
Bovine TB, 27
Buzzards, 156

Cage-type Rat Trap, 141, 145
Carrion Crow, 117-118
Clap-Trap, 141
Crow Trap (Cage), 141
Cyanide Gas, 78, 79, 95

Digging-out, 62, 83
Diseases (ferret), 38

Equipment (ferreting), 65, 71, 87

Fenn Traps, 94, 133-135
Ferrets, breeding, 41
    buying, 29
    care of, young, 42
    Courts, 34
    feeding, 36, 87
    handling, 42, 61
    training, 61–65
Fitch, 16
Fitchet, 16
Foumart, 16

Gassing (badgers), 28
Gassing (rabbits), 94, 95
Gin-trap, 94, 130
Grey Squirrel, 107–108, 151, 153

Hedgehog, 109–112
Holt, 21, 24
Humane Traps, 130–131
Hutch, 32

Jay, 124–127

Kits, 21

Liner, 62, 86
Long-netting, 94
Lost ferrets, 85

Magpie, 121–124
Mole, 112–116, 153
Myxomatosis, 45, 47, 49, 53, 78

Net-Traps, 135, 141, 147
Netting, 65
Night shooting, 96, 100

Otter, 19
Otter-hunting, 22

Pine Marten, 17
Poison, 58
Pole-trap, 129–130
Polecat, 16

Rabbit recipes, 88
Rabbit traps, 134–135
"Rabbit Valley", 51
Rabbits, 45, 54
Rabbiting, 71–78, 80, 86
Rats, 58, 65, 151
Ratting, 100–103
Rook, 119–121

Sable, 19
Safety, 74
Sea-otter, 21
Snaring, 77, 91
Stoat, 11

Terriers, 102
Trapping rabbits, 75
Traps, maintenance of, 150–151
Tunnel-trapping, 146
Tunnels, making, 147
    siting, 148

Vermin-gibbets, 153, 155–156

Warreners, 75
Weasel, 7